# Christianity
# and
# Social Order

WILLIAM TEMPLE

# Christianity
# and
# Social Order

Foreword by The Rt Hon.
EDWARD HEATH, MBE MP

Introduction by the Rev. Canon
RONALD H. PRESTON

SHEPHEARD–WALWYN

First published by Penguin Books 1942
This edition published 1976 by
Shepheard-Walwyn (Publishers) Ltd
15 Alder Road, London SW14 8ER
in association with SPCK

Reprinted 1987 by Shepheard-Walwyn

ISBN -13: 978-0-85683-025-9
ISBN -10: 0-85683-025-9

# *Contents*

# *Foreword*

The impact of William Temple on my generation was immense. When I went up to Balliol in 1935 his mission to Oxford of 1931 was still vividly remembered and widely discussed. His personal influence was not limited to those of his own way of thinking. It extended to those who held no religious belief and to those whose political views did not march with his own. It embraced the whole spectrum of those who were seriously concerned with the social, economic and political problems of his day.

The reason was not far to seek. William Temple was foremost among the leaders of the nation, temporal or spiritual, in posing challenging, radical questions about the nature of our society and its economic basis at a time of world recession, massive unemployment and social despair. The questions he put were specific, those encountered in the everyday lives of ordinary working men and women. He sometimes produced constructive answers, though often of a tentative nature. But whatever the answers to his questions might prove to be, they had to be founded, he insisted, on a moral code. Most important of all, he propounded with lucidity and vigour his understanding of the Christian ethic in its application to the contemporary problems which engrossed us all. Perhaps it was this, more than anything, which appealed to a generation anxiously searching for principles by which to govern its conduct, both private and public. In short, for us he was relevant —when very few others were.

*Christianity and Social Order* embodies William Temple's approach to these matters. Its republication during a period of doubt and questioning not unlike that of the thirties is timely. It enables us to assess how far we have been better able to meet the requirements of a civilized society over the last forty years and to what degree we have fallen short. It is possible for us to identify the features of contemporary life which either went unrecognized or posed no problems for our predecessors. It brings home to every one of us the continuing importance, not so much of having cut-and-dried schemes ready for each eventuality as of being able to rely on a body of principle by which our plans and our actions can be both motivated and judged.

Looking back over nearly half a century, some may feel that in his search for a fairer society William Temple placed too little emphasis on the need to maintain personal freedom; that in his wish to redress the balance of power between those who own and those who produce he failed to see that in so doing some would seek not justice but power for themselves for its own sake; that in his early desire to help the underdog—nowhere better exemplified than in his support for the Workers' Educational Association from which I once benefited—he too readily accepted that his objectives could only be achieved through the Labour Party rather than by setting out to galvanize sympathizers into action in their own parties wherever they could be found in the body politic.

All this may well be true; but the strength of William Temple's broad approach remains. It is the responsibility of the Church to set out its own teaching. It must do so in modern terms. Young people today, as well as many of their elders, are clamouring for an intellectual justification for belief and for the presentation of a morality which is not preoccupied with sexuality but which is relevant to the myriad problems besetting the individual in his personal, his family and his communal activities.

The Church can challenge the existing order with its questions. As William Temple pointed out, others—and particularly in the more technological world in which we now live—may be better able to produce the answers. Only the Church can provide the contemporary teaching, the enunciation of principle, on which all else must be founded. That was William Temple's lasting message. It is fitting that it should be brought to us again in his own words today.

EDWARD HEATH

HOUSE OF COMMONS
LONDON SW1
*12th April 1976*

# Introduction
## Thirty-five Years Later;
## 1941–1976

This book originally appeared as a Penguin Special in 1942, but the Preface was dated November 15th, 1941, when William Temple was still Archbishop of York. By April of the next year he had become Archbishop of Canterbury. In May the book was reprinted and again in August. Soon it had sold well over 150,000 copies. There were further reprints, and in 1956 it was issued as a Pelican, but it has been unobtainable for a number of years. My own copy of the original edition has nearly disintegrated with use and has been preserved from total collapse by being kept in one of the Penguin cellophane covers. A re-issue of it deserves our unqualified welcome, both because it is a key piece of writing in British Christianity this century, and also because no book has as yet replaced it. One is urgently needed, but in its absence we cannot do better than make a serious re-appraisal of *Christianity and Social Order*. I will attempt (i) to locate the book in the national context of 1941 and of Temple's own outlook, (ii) to draw attention to some salient points in the book, (iii) to reflect on what has happened since 1941, with the aim of suggesting what in its approach is of continuing significance.

I

There is little doubt that *Christianity and Social Order* represents a summary of views which Temple had held in general, if not in detail, for most of his working life, but the occasion of its publication was a growing sense in the country at large that a time of war should be a time of reformation; that the enormous effort to overcome the monstrous evil of Nazism, which taxed the British to the uttermost, should be followed—and the British did not allow themselves to entertain the idea that it might not be successful—by a 'new deal'. It was the time of the Beveridge Report with its call for a war against the five giants of want, disease, ignorance, squalor and idleness. In 1943 Temple was to take the chair at a meeting addressed by Beveridge on these matters. It was a developing conviction in the country, which led to the victory of the Labour Party in the General Election of 1945, and the creation of the kind of 'welfare state' in which we still live. It is true that adumbrations of it go back to the Liberal victory at the 1905 election, and perhaps further, but few would deny that the years from 1945 were the decisive ones in its history. Temple's influence in this respect was powerful, as was recognized at the time. The Italian theologian Ernesto Buonauti writing in *La Nuova Europa* in 1945, held that the Archbishop's involvement in the Labour Movement diverted it from more revolutionary outlets. This was to over-simplify. Even if Morgan Phillips' remark that the Labour Movement owed more to Methodism than to Marx is added, it would still be an over-simplification. The point was better put by Denys Munby of Nuffield College, Oxford in *God and the Rich Society* (1960), when he describes *Christianity and Social Order* as 'one of the foundation piers of the Welfare State' (p. 157).

As far as Temple himself was concerned, the immediate context of the book was the Malvern Conference on 'The Life of the Church and the Order of Society', called by him in January 1941. This was stimulating but incoherent, in that the two main groups behind the organization of it did not agree in their diagnosis. One held that the main task was a frontal attack on current economic institutions in favour of common ownership, and the other that it was a theological critique, largely based on the doctrine of Natural Law, leading to economic institutions of a different kind from that advocated by any of the political parties. Even Temple's genius as a Chairman could not bring coherence into the proceedings. It was in this same year that Temple was asked to write a companion Penguin volume to that by the Bishop of Chichester, G. K. A. Bell, on

*Christianity and World Order* (1940). This book is the result. It is a conscious tract for the times, little longer than many pamphlets, and shorter than some, and yet covering a reasonable range of ground. Temple was only to return once more in print to this theme before his death in 1944, and that was a supplement to the *Christian News Letter* of December 29th, 1943 (subsequently reprinted as a pamphlet), on 'What Christians stand for in the Secular World'.

This present book was obviously and inevitably written in haste. There is a certain looseness in construction; for instance love and justice only make their appearance, and that a brief one, at the beginning of the chapter dealing with the Natural Order. There are also some incautious phrases, for instance that Calvinism was 'the mainspring of unrestricted enterprise and competition' (p. 55), but no useful purpose is served by a dissection of these now. Temple himself remarks (p. 76) that he found it hard to write about Christianity and Social Order without writing about everything else at the same time, and I have the same difficulty with this introduction. In the book Temple is consciously addressing a much wider public than usual in his books, and he wants (i) to vindicate the Church's right and duty to 'intervene' on these issues, (ii) to show that it has something worthwhile to say, and (iii) to indicate clearly where the competence of the Church ceases because the issues at that level involve technicalities where she has no special competence. It is for this reason that he separates most of his own particular proposals in an Appendix so that their merits could be assessed independently of his main argument. In my view he is successful in this separation, though he does not show sufficiently clearly how one proceeds from his basic foundations to his particular proposals. To do so would involve a discussion of what are sometimes known by the forbidding term of 'middle axioms', which lie behind what he says on p. 58 but are not explicitly referred to, though Temple is well aware of the problem and the term, as his introduction to the report of the Malvern Conference, *Malvern 1941*, makes clear.[1]

[1] I have discussed middle axioms in Christian social ethics in an article in *Crucible*, the journal of the Board of Social Responsibility of the Church of England, January 1971.

In brief, middle axioms are an attempt to proceed from the basic ethical stance deriving from a theological or philosophical world-view to the realm of the empirical by seeing if there is a consensus among those with *relevant experience* of the matter under discussion (both 'experts' and 'lay' folk) as to the broad moral issued raised, and the *general direction* in which social change should be worked for, without getting as far as *detailed* policies. These in most cases involve so many uncertainties of interpretation of evidence and estimates of possible consequences that it is most unlikely that a Church as a whole, or any Church group of any size, will agree. At this level Christian men and women must use their own judgement as workers and as citizens and, as Temple says, nine-tenths of effective Christian impact on the social order is to be found here and not in Church pronouncements or the activities of ecclesiastical bodies or persons as such (p. 39). Nevertheless, middle axioms, if available, are a help to the formation of the mind of a Christian, and it is at this level that most of the ecumenical social study, which has been such a notable feature of the last fifty years, has for the most part operated.

It was his concern for the witness of the Church as such which made Temple anxious to speak in the main body of the book not in a personal capacity, but to voice 'the main trend of Christian social teaching', to quote his Preface. He goes back to the Old Testament, to the Fathers, to St. Thomas Aquinas and (less confidently) to the Reformers. He draws a great deal on R. H. Tawney's *Religion and the Rise of Capitalism* (1926) and on the symposium edited in 1913 by Bishop Charles Gore, *Property: its Duties and Rights*, both indispensable books still. Tawney is among those to whom Temple expresses special thanks for commenting on the typescript, whilst J. M. Keynes read the galley proofs. Temple was haunted by the charge that it was improper for the Church to 'interfere' in these matters, a charge which is still resurrected though with ever diminishing credibility. It remains true, however, that if the Church supports established institutions it usually passes without comment; it is when she criticizes them that the charge of interference is heard. Keynes' reply is so interesting that it is worth quoting at length from F. A. Iremonger's biography, *William Temple* (p. 438).

'I should have thought that in Chapter I you understated your case. Along one line of origin at least, economics more properly called political economy is on the side of ethics. Marshall always used to insist that it was through ethics that he arrived at political economy and I would claim myself in this, as in other respects, to be a pupil of his. I should have thought that nearly all English economists in the tradition, apart from Ricardo, reached economics that way. There are practically no issues of policy as distinct from technique which do not involve ethical considerations. If this is emphasized, the right of the Church to interfere in what is essentially a branch of ethics becomes even more obvious.

I should have thought again that you were understating your case in the third chapter, where you consider the past record of the Church in these matters. I should have supposed that it was a very recent heresy indeed to cut these matters out of its province. Are you not going too far in suggesting that in the XVIII Century the Church accepted this limitation? I should have thought decidedly not. Leaving out the Scots, such as Hume and Adam Smith, and foreign residents in London, such as Mandeville and Cantillon, I can think of no one important in the development of politico-economic ideas, apart from Bentham, who was not a clergyman and in most cases a high dignitary of the Church. For example, Dean Swift interested himself in these matters. Bishop Fleetwood wrote the first scientific treatise on price and the theory of index numbers. Bishop Berkeley wrote some of the shrewdest essays in these subjects available in his time. Bishop Butler, although primarily of ethical importance, is not to be neglected in this field. Archdeacon Paley is of fundamental importance. The Reverend T. R. Malthus was the greatest economist writing in the XVIII Century after Adam Smith. I agree that unless one includes Laud there are not many Archbishops before yourself to be included in the list. But Archbishop Sumner's early work was on economics.'

The point made by Keynes in his second paragraph is, of course, rather a different one from that which was Temple's concern. Keynes is referring to Church dignitaries who made themselves masters of the subject of political economy as it was at the time, and actually made contributions to its development. That could not be said of Temple, and in any event it would be much more difficult to do in our age of much greater specialization. The Church of England has produced a handful of dignitaries trained in the natural sciences, but not a single one as yet trained in the social sciences. Temple was well informed on social issues but not in the field of economics and the social sciences as such. He was well aware of this, but it led him to take too seriously, especially in the last years of his life, some Christians who wrote so much and so critically about economics, that people tended to assume that they must have been qualified in it and knew what they were talking about, and indeed that they were proposing pathbreaking advances in the subject. In fact none of them were qualified in it, and it led them and those who were influenced by them into many elementary errors. J. S. Carmichael and H. S. Goodwin in their *William Temple's Political Legacy* (1963), have no difficulty in showing some of Temple's errors, but the effect of their book is lessened by their naïve enthusiasm for liberalism in the narrow sense of *laissez-faire* and free competition; and the large number of competent economists who are also castigated by them leaves the reader feeling that Temple is in good company. The other book on the subject, *Social Concern in the Thought of William Temple*, by Robert Craig (1963), now Principal of the University College of Rhodesia, is in fact much stronger on the theological parts of his thought. A thorough survey of Temple's social teaching remains to be written.

The immediate roots of this social teaching were (i) Anglican Incarnational Theology from the time of F. D. Maurice through such thinkers as B. F. Westcott, Scott Holland and Charles Gore, (ii) the Ecumenical Movement from its earliest beginnings in the COPEC Conference at Birmingham in 1924 (on Politics, Education and Citizenship), of which Temple was Chairman, and which was itself a British preparation for the 'Life and Work' Conference at Stockholm in 1925. He was prominent in the Oxford Conference on 'Church, Community and State' of 1937, and as a result came into touch with the social teaching of Emil Brunner, and especially Reinhold Niebuhr, (iii) the Christendom Group in the Church of

England, which at that time sponsored a journal of that name and an annual summer school of 'Christian Sociology' at Oxford; it particularly stressed the doctrine of Natural Law. Something needs to be said about each of these three:

(i) The Anglican Incarnational tradition in Theology can conveniently be studied in Archbishop Ramsey's *From Gore to Temple* (1960). This is not the occasion to explore it in detail, nor to defend every aspect of it (for example from the charge that its doctrine of the Trinity verged on tritheism), nor to set much store by its confessional source. Its strength from our present concern is the forcible way it expressed a positive attitude to this world which must follow from the belief that 'the Word was made flesh', and brought a certain type of otherworldly pietist Christianity under critical scrutiny as verging on heresy. But we must not make too much of this. Richard Niebuhr's *Christ and Culture* (1950) has convincingly shown that a 'Christ against Culture' attitude is one of five stances which have continually re-appeared in the Christian Church and which, whilst by no means adequate as a complete expression of the relation of Christianity to this world, at critical points is cogent and powerful. Also we need to remember that the key Christian doctrines link together, so that it is possible to reach a positive attitude to this world from all of them—Creation, Atonement, the Church, the Sacraments, the Last Things (to take a traditional division)—and not merely from the Incarnation. Temple shows this in this book. A certain blandness characterized the outlook of exponents of Incarnational Theology on the social order, which underplayed the extent of the injustices, tensions and conflicts to be found in it. Association with the Ecumenical Movement brought Temple into touch with different strains, with theologians who objected to the turning of the great themes of Christian Theology arising out of the events of Christ's life, death and resurrection into social 'principles'. It was consciousness of this which led Temple in his *Christian Newsletter* supplement to urge the necessity of digging deeper theological foundations and of being content with a less grandiose superstructure.

(ii) The influence of the incipient Ecumenical Movement was as

great as his influence on it. Reinhold Niebuhr is the key figure here.
Both he and Temple were equally prominent in the Oxford
Conference. The fourth of the six volumes of essays published in
1938 on the theme of the Conference consists of essays by seven
theologians on the overall theme, 'Christian Faith and the
Common Life'. The third is by Temple (the fourth by Niebuhr), and
it represents what is in many ways a shorter, trial run for *Christianity
and Social Order*, and is a more taut and powerful piece. Further,
the influence of J. H. Oldham on Temple was considerable. He and
W. A. Visser 't Hooft edited a preparatory volume for the
Conference, *The Church and its Function in Society*, and his section is
frequently reflected in this present book. So is the report of Section
3 of the Conference, 'Church, Community and State in Relation to
the Economic Order', which is probably the best of the six sectional
reports of the Conference, and the only one to be reprinted
separately in addition to its inclusion in the book of the proceedings
of the Conference, *The Churches Survey their Task*. It is one of the great
documents of Christian Social Ethics in this century, and
considerably in advance, for example, of where the Papal Social
Encyclicals had got by this time.

(iii) The element of the Natural Law tradition in Temple's thought
is even more difficult to deal with briefly than that of the Middle
Axioms. Christians are divided between those to whom the term is
familiar, even though their understanding of it and its implications
varies considerably, and those to whom it is unknown or
meaningless or theologically suspect. Indeed one of the most
cogent reflections on it known to me is the sentence in the
Introduction to the book, *Natural Law* (1951) by A. P. d'Entrèves,
which refers to it as a notion 'laden with ambiguity even in the days
when it was considered self-evident'. It is true that there has been
some revival of Natural Law thinking, in the sense of holding that
the making of moral judgements is 'natural' to man and part of
what it distinctively means to be a human being. (This is what the
Bible presupposes as much as it presupposes God.) It is also an
affirmation that in making moral judgements men should not, and
at their best do not, merely reflect their tastes and prejudices or

those of their family, group or society, but are responding to what is the case, to a good and a right transcending their own. If someone makes the judgement 'Hitler was a bad man' he is stating what simply is the case.

But the doctrine of Natural Law has traditionally been used in a different way. It has been held that there is something fixed in 'nature' which man can perceive and to which he must conform, and which can be deduced from some general principle, or from the 'nature' of an act devoid of any particular human context. In this sense the doctrine has taken hard knocks recently. The heirs of those who used it most are now increasingly questioning it. Roman Catholic Moral Theology has undergone what can only be called a revolutionary change in the last twenty years. It is possible that this traditional use of the doctrine in the Papal Encyclical *Humanae Vitae* may be the last instance of it. Unfortunately it was this use that Temple adopted in his last years. It is reflected in this book, but on examination we can see that it is marginal to his argument. He tells us (p. 80) in a loosely written paragraph that the Natural Law or Order is discovered 'partly by observing generally accepted standards of judgement' (a statement which needs clarification, for one cannot tell whether he refers to the basic moral insight of man as such or to something more restricted), and 'partly by consideration of the proper function of whatever is the subject of enquiry', and that this is apprehended 'by a consideration of its own nature'. The chief conclusion he draws from this is that production exists for consumption and not *vice versa*. A first reflection is that it hardly needs a considerable theological apparatus to establish that goods and services are produced in order to be consumed. This is, of course, the lynch pin of the pure *laissez-faire* theory of capitalism, according to which the consumer is king. (It is not clear whether Temple realized this; I think not.) The practice, however, has been markedly different.[2] But apart from the difference between practice and theory, the principle is too simple to resolve the diverse

[2] This is constantly being pointed out. An exposition in a contemporary context is that of the distinguished Harvard economist J. K. Galbraith, who writes so readably that he can command Pelican editions of his books. His *Economics and the Public Purpose*, is a recent example.

conflicts in society. We have different interests as producers and consumers; and most of us have divided interests, in that over a small area we are producers and over a large one consumers; and as producers we may be consumers of raw materials or partially manufactured ones and producers of a finished product. Certainly consumers' interests need attention, and the recent moves by the Government and by a private body like the Consumers' Association to pay them more attention is to be welcomed, but it is too simple to say that in all conflicts of interest those of the consumers must carry most weight. To take one illustration, the National Coal Board has greatly reduced the number of persons engaged in coal mining since nationalization, and it has done it in a gradual and humane way without throwing individuals and communities on the scrap heap. However, it has only been possible because the rest of us have paid more for our coal than otherwise we would have done. And this was right.

Much of the concern lying behind the revived interest in Natural Law has now passed into ecumenical studies of the human (or the Humanum as it is often somewhat grandiloquently called), notably that headed by Canon David Jenkins from 1969 to 1973. It is interesting that the same concern has been reflected in folk songs in recent years. Man must respect nature, in the sense in which a sculptor must respect the nature of his material, but he is not a servant of it but a creative manipulator of it. He is challenged to achieve his full humanity in the world, to be truly human. We do not know all that he has in him to become. His potentialities will be further explored and achieved by negative judgements on the *status quo*, as we shall shortly see, and by acting on them as a basis for guiding social change; they are not developed by issuing *a priori* commands and prohibitions in the name of Natural Law as has so often been done in the past.


II


The central concern of Temple in this book is indeed that of the human. From basic Christian beliefs about God and man he draws what he calls primary and secondary principles. The primary one amounts to respect for persons, or rather the person-in-community, because of the inherently social character of man. With Jacques Maritain he draws a sharp distinction between the person and the individual, and influenced by them I have for a long time striven to banish the term individual from my Christian vocabulary. John Macmurray was later to expound this point in his own way in his Gifford Lectures of 1953 and 1954, *The Self as Agent*, and *Persons in Relation*, adumbrations of which had appeared in his *Freedom in the Modern World* in the decade before Temple's Penguin. It has also, of course, an obvious relation to the thought of Kant, and indeed that of J. S. Mill, but it was not from these sources, nor the Oxford idealist philosophy of the late nineteenth century that Temple took it, but from Christian theology. Nevertheless, they helped , as other philosophies at different times have helped in other ways Christians to draw from their faith insights which were latent but not fully realized.

In the course of his exposition, Temple skilfully brings in four rather different points. (i) The fact that respect for persons does not mean an idealized view of them, but seeing them as they are in their sin as well as their grandeur. This leads him to the most effective popular exposition of that doctrine confusingly called 'original sin' which I have ever read (p. 60). (ii) That the working of this principle in the social order is by a negative judgement on aspects of the *status quo*. I am sure this is right and it is important. We do not as Christians have a blueprint of an ideal social order; we are led to look at the present situation in the light of our Christian understanding of life and identify those aspects which particularly offend it, and say 'this won't do'. Then we have to get down to the detailed task of how to achieve change in the right direction. (iii) In dealing in politics with men as they are and not as they ought to be Temple arrives at a splendid 'realist' sentence. 'The art of Government in fact is the art of so ordering life that self-interest prompts what justice demands' (p. 65). The far-reaching implications of this are worth pondering. (iv) He brings out that the person is largely what he is because he is born into 'social units' which profoundly affect him, especially before he is consciously aware of them. He refers to the family and the nation. These are not 'deliberately manufactured structures' (p. 64) but 'the product of historical development'. Temple does not give any theological support for this, but he could have aptly done so by referring to the Reformation doctine of the 'Orders of Creation'. I should have been happier if he had cited the state rather than the nation, for on examination the nation proves to be all too uncertain a concept to be given such basic status, whereas the political order of the state is fundamental. There are issues here too large to take up, but important because of the frequent identification in the modern world of Christianity with nationalism, and the fact that acquiescing in this or fostering it in each country is the easiest way for the Church to be popular. The main point here is that the recognition of the basic importance of these 'social units' shows the folly of the argument frequently mooted as to whether Christians should be concerned with changing persons or changing structures. Both are equally important, for both influence the other for good or ill. In terms of this book we can see how important it is that structures should be humane and just because of their effect on persons.

The chapter on derivative principles mentions freedom, social fellowship and service. This leads Temple to stress the importance of intermediate groups, so that neither overall individualism nor collectivism is a satisfactory position. Here Papal Encyclicals are drawn on, from which the principle of subsidiarity might have been mentioned, that is to say that wider authorities should not take on what can adequately be discharged by more local ones (*Quadragesimo Anno*, 1931, par. 80). In fact today we have the hard task of devising both wider and more local ones at the same time, from the Common Market to the neighbourhood. He also stresses the place of minorities, and mentions the role of Dissent in British life. He might well have referred in this connection to two short books by A. D. Lindsay, *The Essentials of Democracy* (1929) and *The Churches and Democracy* (1934), which have been neglected lately. A further point of political importance is the necessity of checking our narrower loyalties by our wider ones, where there is much to be said for which Temple had no space. He qualifies the point by an illustration which seems to me to go too far on the 'realist side'. 'If a man applies in the training of his children standards *not generally accepted in their circle* (my italics), and fails to bring the children themselves to accept them, the result is likely to be an alienation of the children, both from their father and from his standards'. (p. 76). The problem is clear, but since one cannot know in advance whether one will bring one's children to challenge currently accepted standards, Temple's proviso seems to lead to a perpetual support of the *status quo*. (The kind of situation which Temple may well have had in mind is that of a parent who lives in social circles where it is customary to opt out of the State system of education and to pay the fees to send children to 'public' schools.)

The particular proposals Temple arrived at are not our special concern now. There is not all that difference between the last chapter, where they are more general, and the Appendix, where they are more detailed. Control of land use, and financial proposals come in the latter. Education figures in both. It is depressing in 1976 to be reminded by Temple in 1941 of what H. A. L. Fisher said in 1918 when introducing the Education Bill of that year, 'Every citizen under the age of eighteen should be regarded as primarily a subject of education, not primarily a factor in industry' (p. 102). For the rest, malnutrition is not what it was; the nation was better fed under war time rationing than it had been in peace time and we have not slipped back. We are also better clothed. Holidays with pay have been achieved; and family allowance after the first child (not the second as Temple advocates). Indeed our standard of living has doubled since this book was written. But housing remains a scandal; long-term unemployment is returning after we thought we had banished it, though the circumstances of those unemployed is much better than it was in the 1930s. Inequalities of wealth and power are still great. A. B. Atkinson's study, *On Equal Shares* (1972) indicated that 91 per cent of the total personal wealth of the country is in the hands of the richest 10 per cent, and 72 per cent in that of 5 per cent (p. 15). True, there are arguments about the calculations of these figures, and we now have a Royal Commission on the Distribution of Income and Wealth, but substantial inequality cannot be gainsaid. And as to power, the responsibility of the worker in industry is still slight. In short, social problems have proved more intractable than we expected. Temple's general attitude seems right. The root of the matter is that the very substance of his faith should make the Christian ask radical questions about his society, whereas throughout Christian history Christians have tended either to accept the political and economic structures as they found them unreflectively, or else explicitly identify them with the will of God.

### III

What has happened since Temple's death which bears on this book? On the theological front I mention five points. (i) It is much more obvious than it was in 1941 that we live in a plural society. This makes his unguarded remark (p. 37) unfortunate, ' . . . apart from faith in God there is really *nothing* (my italics) to be said for the notion of human equality'. Belief in God in the Judaeo-Christian tradition is undoubtedly a strong support for such a belief, and support can be found in other religions, but there are many atheists and agnostics in our society, and it is important that the search for a common morality to undergird the respect for persons should include the widest possible range of beliefs. Our time has seen efforts of public bodies like the United Nations and private ones like Amnesty International to work in this area. Undoubtedly their work is fragile; all the more reason to support it. (ii) There has been the growth of Industrial Chaplaincies, so that there are far more in industry who have been specifically helped to relate the Christian faith to industry than when Temple wrote. Surprisingly little of the thinking of 'Industrial Mission' has as yet appeared in print, but it surely will before long. This growth is part of the much greater stress in the Church on the role of the laity, exactly as Temple wished, though one would like to see more signs of that laity in evidence in industry. (iii) The Ecumenical Movement has grown enormously. A Temple writing today could draw on the work of the Geneva Conference of 1966 on 'Christians in the Technical and Social Revolutions of our Time'. It was designed to achieve in its time what the Oxford Conference did in 1937. In 1966 there was a wider frame of reference. It was the most truly ecumenical conference on Christian social ethics ever held, and this made the radical stance it took all the more significant, for it showed that when the more 'established' white Churches were no longer so predominant, the radical stance which Temple exemplified came to the fore.[3] Perhaps even more significant, since it was in a sense unofficial, was the fact that the official Assembly of the World Council of Churches meeting at Uppsala two years later did not repudiate it but broadly endorsed it. The new radical notes which came to the fore for the first time in general ecumenical Christian social ethics (together with old ones from Oxford and earlier) have become pervasive since then. Also there has been the *aggiornamento* in the Roman Catholic Church initiated by Pope John XXIII, particularly focused in the second Vatican Council, 1962–5. For the first time such a Council dealt with the themes covered in the Pastoral Constitution *Gaudium et Spes* (The Church in the Modern World), with results remarkably similar to what was to be the line of the Geneva Conference. Since the Council there has been the Papal Encyclical *Populorum Progressio*, and the Apostolic Letter of Pope Paul VI to Cardinal Roy, President of the Pontifical Commission for Justice and Peace, *Octogesima Adveniens*, on the eightieth anniversary of the Encyclical *Rerum Novarum* which is the foundation of the modern Roman Catholic social teaching. (iv) We are now much more used to thinking of the Church sociologically. Indeed the Sociology of Religion as an academic study has had a revival, in the sense of returning to a major pre-occupation of the founding fathers of sociology like Durkheim and Weber. This means that the social effects of the Church as an institution, and of its internal structure, are looked at more explicitly. So the question of the Church's involvement—and especially how it should 'interfere'—can be discussed with more realism. (v) There has been the development of a 'political theology' with its various aspects, of which the theologies of hope and liberation, or revolutionary theology as it is sometimes called, are the most significant. One side of theologies of liberation is the acceptance of Marxist categories, a

[3] I have dealt with this more fully in the first chapter of a book I edited in 1971, *Technology and Social Justice*, covering the years 1966–8 in ecumenical social ethics.

point to which I shall return; on the theological side the strongly eschatological emphasis is a further illustration that radical and positive stances towards this world can be drawn from all aspects of Christian doctrine.

I turn now to six points on the political and social front since Temple's death.

(i) The toughness of some social problems has already been mentioned. Others include the fact that we have made hardly any dint in the relative deprivation of the lower-paid worker, that a lot of school leavers go into dead-end jobs, and at the moment are not in a job at all; that the numbers on Supplementary Benefit do not fall; and that there is much evidence of harm to children in deprived families.

(ii) The conditions of employment in industry have considerably improved both in themselves, and in terms of redundancy and re-training. The Employment Protection Act which came into force this year will improve things further. But little progress has been made (though more in West Germany, Austria, Denmark, Norway, Sweden and Holland) towards what Temple emphasized so strongly, industrial democracy, or the right of the workers not merely to be informed about, but to be consulted and to participate in, deciding about the conditions of their work and the policies of the company they work for. These issues seem now to be coming to the front; it remains to be seen what we shall do about them. I cannot help reflecting ruefully that the first time I ventured into print after graduating was in a study booklet on these issues, and more than a generation later I read in *The Economist* of January 11th, 1975, an article advocating precisely the same thing, which pointed out that until very recently they have been ignored in Britain, and that while they can be evaded for some time they cannot be put off for ever. For 'the need for participation was created by society, not invented by sociologists, right-wing trade unionists, or capitalists trying to breathe new life into a supposedly dying system'; it added that society is 'ever more inclined to contest decisions taken from on high, ever more educated, and frequently competent to do so. This is true of the shop floor, of white-collar workers, of every level of management.'

(iii) We have discovered the third and fourth worlds in a way and on a scale unmatched a generation ago. The third world has forced itself on our attention by providing the first instance of economic power—oil power—against a wealthy 'west' which has been used to dictating its own terms of trade. The fourth world on the other hand has forced itself on our attention by its very misery. Modern means of mass communication have brought this before us in a way hitherto unknown. We are the first generation to hear the cry of the suffering expressed from every corner of the world, and knowledge brings responsibility. It has become more obvious how inter-dependent we are, and according to our economic and political power so we affect the lives of others or are affected ourselves by the decisions of others. This is a reality which governments and electorates would rather forget, and one which demands greater skill and wisdom from both.

(iv) Inflation is an issue which Temple did not have to face. If it continues at anything like 15 per cent to 25 per cent per annum for any number of years it will be more disruptive of the social system than a world war. Much of it is due to international factors, but much also depends upon the ability with which it is handled domestically. The crucial issue to be faced is that no government can combine three things, all of which many people would like: a stable price level, full employment, and free collective bargaining. They are incompatible. What social policies provide the best 'mix' is the issue before western type democracies.

(v) The easy way out of this dilemma has been thought to be the pursuit of greater affluence. This still has a contribution to make. The advocates of no growth have overstated the case. But they have drawn attention to the need for much more caution and care. Moreover what we do with our wealth becomes an ever more pressing question in the 'one world' of today.

(vi) If there are some things it is inherently impossible for governments to do, there are others which are politically impossible. They can adopt in a depression Keynesian policies of tax rebates and increased public spending. This is popular, and it has been effective. But in a boom they cannot deflate by increasing taxes and cutting public expenditure because powerful large companies (some multinational) and trade unions are against it. And society is equally opposed to the other policy of cutting the money supply because it is not prepared to accept the level of unemployment that would ensue. If an open society like ours is to survive it will demand more state activity in promoting public bargaining which relates consumption and investment to resources and productivity. Possibly annual synchronized wage negotiations together with some price restrictions will be needed as part of the most suitable political 'mix'. Evidence from Sweden may be helpful here.

This brings me to the British political tradition. We have had a long continuity of political and social institutions because the gradual break up of medieval structures prepared the way for the British to lead in the development of industry, and thus become wealthy. Time and wealth have been on our side. Nor have we had our institutions forcefully disrupted by foreign invasion. As a result we have developed considerable political skills in government and in social and industrial processes. Can we continue to change smoothly?

One element in our tradition, and how far it is cause and how far effect is probably an unanswerable question, is a strong moral element derived from the Christian faith. Elements in it include (i) medieval social thought continuing to the seventeenth century and picked up in the nineteenth, which powerfully influenced Temple; (ii) radical Dissent and political offshoots from it; (iii) the spin-off from the Methodist movement, particularly in its Primitive Methodist form; (iv) more recently the urban working class Roman Catholic element in the Labour Party. This moral element has tended to mitigate social conflicts where a more Marxist frame of thought exacerbates them. Reinhold Niebuhr had a very interesting editorial on this in the journal *Christianity and Society* in the summer of 1943 (Vol. 8 No. 3).[4] He was discussing, among other things, the

---

[4] I am reminded of this—for I was in fact the British agent for the journal at the time—by a research student of mine, Mr. J. R. Atherton, M.A., of the William Temple Foundation, to whom I am also much indebted for the reference to Buonauti, and for discussing this introduction with me in the light of two unpublished papers by him, 'William Temple and Politics', and 'The Reconstruction of the British Christian Social Tradition'.

significance of England having as Archbishop of Canterbury a man with social views as radical as those of Temple. 'In other words the moral protest against the injustices of our society is derived from, and need not express itself against, the Christian Religion. This one fact makes Britain unique in modern social history. For all the radical movements of the Continent have been anti-Christian. In America they are not anti-Christian but they are predominantly secular. It may be that the unbroken character of the Christian ethos in Britain is also the cause of the unbroken socio-political history since 1688.' But he went on to point out the defect of this virtue, that Britain 'may well maintain many forms of capitalistic injustice because of her ability to mitigate them more successfully than other nations'.

The biggest challenge to this whole way of thinking comes from the Liberation and Revolutionary Theology of Latin America. A good survey can be found in *Revolutionary Theology Comes of Age*, by José Míguez Bonino (1975). In the last resort it depends on accepting the broad validity of a Marxian analysis. Whether it is true for Latin America is not our present business. If it is there is no *theological* reason to deny the revolutionary, political and economic conclusions of so many Latin American theologians.[5] I do not think it is true for Britain, though the question cannot be dealt with here. However, a question which ought to be considered is whether Temple in *Christianity and Social Order* should have more explicitly linked his conclusions to socialism. After all in his youth he did. In an article in *The Economic Review* in 1908 (Vol. XVIII, p. 199) he says 'The alternative stands before us—socialism or heresy. . . . In other words, Socialism . . . is the economic realization of the Christian Gospel.' It is sometimes said that later in life he moved to the Right politically, and it is true that he did not continue to express himself in this way. But it could be held that the radical questions in *Christianity and Social Order* point that way, and it might be asked

[5] Certainly it is not possible to put *order* so unequivocally as the first political requisite as Temple does (p. 61), because we have become much more conscious of the 'established disorder' of many political systems, and of the 'institutional violence' expressed in many ostensibly powerful structures.

whether it was anything more than diplomatic caution which
prevented him saying so, perhaps akin to the reasons which made
him give up his membership of the Labour Party in 1921, after three
years in it.

To this four points may be made.

(i) The Christian criticism of capitalism, echoing F. D. Maurice,
on the grounds that competition is a lie, and that we should have
production for use and not for profit, is much too simple, as
Temple clearly sees in this book. It is rather the institutional
structures within which competition is carried on and private
property dealt with that need scrutiny.

(ii) The political case for socialism in the old sense of 'the
nationalization of all the means of production, distribution and
exchange' has been clouded by the evidence from Russia and her
satellites of the dangers of monolithic power structures; and the
evidence of communist countries like Jugoslavia or China which in
their different ways are trying alternative structures is, so far,
ambiguous and not sufficient to clear doubts.

(iii) Keynesian economic policies overthrew the expectation,
widely held in the 1930s, that the capitalist system was breaking
down, as the Marxian analysis said it would. Our present difficulties
do not show that it must break down, though there is always the
possibility that it may do so if enough political wisdom is not shown
by governments and electorates in dealing with it. If it does, the
result will be a much less open society than the one we have
experienced and—I would say—enjoy.

(iv) There has been an utopianism pervasive in the Labour
Movement, associated with a belief in evolutionary progress based
on the spread of education. This has become less plausible, and its
decline has left many in that movement in something of a spiritual
vacuum. The utopian belief was an off-shoot of the Christian-
humanist tradition, and it served as a surrogate for a religious faith.
If that has faded, and Marxism with its religious overtones does not
seem plausible, a certain emptiness is left; for whatever may be the
case with right-wing political movements, a cynical realism (which
may appear all that is left as an option) does not go well with left-
wing ones. Temple stands for a Christian realism as in various

places in this book he implicitly addresses himself to the situation I have described.

There remains his concern for equality for the sake of human fellowship. It lies behind the socialist case and in Temple's view it lies near the heart of the Christian gospel. It leads to the asking of radical questions about the social order. This Temple did. His questions remain as relevant as when he asked them, even though the empirical background is in many respects different. In dealing with them the question of how far the state should control production is a valid but subsidiary one. It is part of a range of questions involving, (a) the powers needed by the state for particular necessary economic functions and the checks needed on the abuse of the power; (b) the type and extent of participation in decision making, and (c) the role of intermediate associations in the light of the principle of subsidiarity.[6]

Among intermediate associations the Churches are of great importance, and this is why Temple's pre-occupation in this book with the Church's involvement (allowing for his stress on the importance of the Christian in his job and as a citizen) remains important. Her method of doing so needs constant reflection, and there has been much ecumenical discussion of this since the Geneva Conference of 1966. I am thinking, for example, of Paul Ramsey's book *Who Speaks for the Churches?* (1967), and the debates on the actions of the World Council of Churches in its Programme to Combat Racism since 1970. Further, the involvement of the Church herself through her ownership and administration of property and investments has come to the fore. The ethics of investment and the social responsibilities of the corporate investor are live issues which will not go away. They have also come to the fore at a time when the Churches have a smaller membership to rely on for regular giving,

[6] Many Christians have not seen this, and adopt an individualistic ethic partly because it is not the focus of the teaching of Jesus, nor was it the focus of the early Church with its belief in the imminent *parousia* and its insignificant position in the Roman Empire. Temple brings the question of the role of groups to the forefront, though he could have spelt out more fully how he related it theologically to his fundamental stress on the status of person.

too much property to maintain and (probably) too many paid personnel, and this at a time of high inflation. How they react to this will be a kind of litmus paper test of their social convictions. For they need to demonstrate by actions as well as by teaching that they are indeed on the side of the disadvantaged, and not only in the sense of 'ambulance work' which deals with disasters, but also in furthering structures which prevent them. These structures need to express man's freedom in fellowship without romanticizing him, so that his selfishness is both contained and utilized. However, the less there is of selfishness the better, so that there is the continued need for personal as well as for social renewal. To promote both is a task of the Church. It follows from her worship of God through Christ her Lord.

RONALD PRESTON

DEPARTMENT OF SOCIAL AND PASTORAL THEOLOGY
THE UNIVERSITY OF MANCHESTER
*Epiphany 1976*

# *Prefatory Note*

It was originally suggested to me that I should write this little book as a companion to the Bishop of Chichester's admirable Penguin volume *Christianity and World Order*. I did not find it possible to follow his method as closely as I should have wished; but as I have been unable to supply so many quotations from official utterances of Church assemblies, I take this opportunity of referring to the Reports of the Lambeth Conferences of 1897, 1908 and 1920; to the relevant section of the Report of the Oxford Conference of 1937; and to the Statement lately issued by the Commission of the Churches for International Friendship and Social Responsibility under the title *Social Justice and Economic Reconstruction*. Reference to these will shew that the principles which I lay down are not an expression of a purely personal point of view but represent the main trend of Christian social teaching.

Apart from all those to whose writings I am indebted I want to thank Miss Dorothy Howell-Thomas who typed the whole book; Professor R. H. Tawney and Miss Alice Lascelles, B.Sc.Econ., who read the typescript and made many valuable suggestions; also Professor B. Mouat Jones, Vice-Chancellor of Leeds University, Professor Henry Clay, and Mr. J. M. Keynes who read the galley proofs and enabled me by their comments to avoid some ambiguities and to improve the argument. It is hardly necessary to add that no one of these has any responsibility for what I say.

WILLIAM EBOR

*November 15th, 1941*

# 1

## *What Right has the Church to Interfere?*

The claim of the Christian Church to make its voice heard in matters of politics and economics is very widely resented, even by those who are Christian in personal belief and in devotional practice. It is commonly assumed that Religion is one department of life, like Art or Science, and that it is playing the part of a busybody when it lays down principles for the guidance of other departments, whether Art and Science or Business and Politics. When a group of Bishops attempted to bring Government, Coal-Owners and Miners together in a solution of the disastrous Coal Strike of 1926, Mr. Baldwin, then Prime Minister, asked how the Bishops would like it if he referred to the Iron and Steel Federation the revision of the Athanasian Creed; and this was acclaimed as a legitimate score.

I

Few people read much history. In an age when it is tacitly assumed that the Church is concerned with another world than this, and in this with nothing but individual conduct as bearing on prospects in that other world, hardly any one reads the history of the Church in its exercise of political influence. It is assumed that the Church exercises little influence and ought to exercise none; it is further assumed that this assumption is self-evident and has always been made by reasonable men. As a matter of fact it is entirely modern and extremely questionable.

Of course, it has a real foundation. No assumption is commonly made without one. The foundation is two-fold, and consists, first, in a perfectly sound conviction that each main department of life is independent and autonomous as regards its own technique, and secondly that the Church in the days of its power, and Christian theorists of a later time, have often ignored this. Just as the theologians interfered with the autonomy of Natural Science on its own ground in the case of Galileo, so they have at times interfered with action in the economic field where technical as well as moral questions were involved. The attempts made by Archbishop Laud to use the Star Chamber as a means of preventing the oppression of the common people by 'engrossing' corn or his eagerness to promote the work of the Commissions established to check 'enclosures', illustrate this. Laud was petulant and arrogant; but he was a friend of the poor with a genuine passion for justice, and a stalwart opponent of that 'progress' which enslaves them. He has been too harshly judged. 'If his vices made him intolerable to the most powerful forces of his own age, his virtues were not of a kind to commend him to those of its successor, and history has been hardly more merciful to him than were his political opponents.'[1]

Laud was no innovator. He was a die-hard conservative. He was trying to conserve the medieval tradition which the great Reformers did not repudiate but rather tried to re-establish. Latimer was quite as much a prophetic upholder of the old moral principles in political economy as a reformer of ecclesiastical doctrine and worship. The control of the Church in this field has never been fully effective, but its law was not a dead letter. 'Florence was the financial capital of medieval Europe; but even at Florence the secular authorities fined bankers right and left in the middle of the fourteenth century.'[2] Two centuries later 'Archbishop Grindal's injunctions to the laity of the Province of York (1571) expressly emphasized the duty of presenting to the Ordinary those who lend and demand back more than the principal, whatever the guise under which the transaction may be concealed.'[3]

It was not till after the Restoration that the Church in England ceased to claim moral control in the field of business. Then there was a rapid retreat upon the central citadel of religion, and during most of the eighteenth century theology and the direct relation of the soul to God were alone regarded as the Church's concern. This could not last. John Wesley had no intention of bringing the Church back into politics, but his revival had that effect. The abolition of the slave trade and of slavery itself were political projects; but they were carried through by Evangelicals in the fervour of their Evangelical faith. It is reported of Lord Melbourne, Queen Victoria's first· Prime Minister, that after hearing an Evangelical preacher he remarked that, if religion was going to interfere with the affairs of private life, things were come to a pretty pass; later Prime Ministers have felt and said the same about the interference of religion with the affairs of public life; but the interference steadily increases and will increase.

It is interesting to note the stages of the recovery. First came the long campaign for the abolition of the slave trade and emancipation of the slaves. This was prompted by human sympathy and care for the individuals affected. It was shortly afterwards followed by the movement for the reform of prisons associated at successive stages with the names of John Howard and Elizabeth Fry. Still the concern was for individuals. Then came the series of Factory Acts; and still the motive was concern for individuals; but now, not only was the action taken political, but it was such as affected the relations between employer and employed, and, to that extent, the structure of society. While that series of Acts was being passed, James Ludlow, soon to be followed by F. D. Maurice and Charles Kingsley, launched the Christian Social Movement, which subjected the whole order of society to criticism in the light of Christian beliefs about God and man. This was carried on by Westcott, Gore and Scott Holland up to the eve of the Four Years' War and into the period following it. Its fullest expression, perhaps, was the Conference on Christian Politics, Economics and Citizenship (COPEC) held at Birmingham in 1924.

This rapid survey of history shows that the claim of the Church today to be heard in relation to political and economic problems is no new usurpation, but a re-assertion of a right once universally admitted and widely regarded. But it also shows that this right may be compromised by injudicious exercise, especially when the 'autonomy of technique' in the various departments of life is ignored. Religion may rightly censure the use of artistic talents for making money out of men's baser tastes, but it cannot lay down laws about perspective or the use of a paint-brush. It may insist that scientific enquiry be prompted by a pure love of truth and not distorted (as in Nazi Germany) by political considerations. It may declare the proper relation of the economic to other activities of men, but it cannot claim to know what will be the purely economic effect of particular proposals. It is, however, entitled to say that some economic gains ought not to be sought because of the injuries involved to interests higher than economic; and this principle of the subordination of the whole economic sphere is not yet generally accepted. We all recognize that in fact the exploitation of the poor, especially of workhouse children, in the early days of power-factories was an abomination not to be excused by any economic advantage thereby secured; but we fail to recognize that such an admission in a particular instance carries with it the principle that economics are properly subject to a non-economic criterion.

II

The approach to the problem in our own time is to be made along four distinct lines: (1) the claims of sympathy for those who suffer; (2) the educational influence of the social and economic system; (3) the challenge offered to our existing system in the name of justice; (4) the duty of conformity to the 'Natural Order' in which is to be found the purpose of God.

(1) The suffering caused by existing evils makes a claim upon our sympathy which the Christian heart and conscience cannot ignore. Before the outbreak of war there were three main causes of wide-spread suffering—bad housing, malnutrition. and unemployment. The varied forms of suffering which bad housing causes are easy to imagine in part, but few who have had no personal knowledge of it are able to imagine the whole—the crushing of a woman's pride in her home through the ceaseless and vain struggle against dirt and squalor; the nervous fret; the lack of home comforts for the tired worker; the absence of any space for

children to play. The bad conditions in slum quarters are not chiefly due to the people living there. When they are moved to new housing estates, more than half of them rise fully to the fresh opportunity, and three-quarters of them make a reasonable use of it. The toleration of bad housing is a wanton and callous cruelty.

Malnutrition is a direct result of poverty and ignorance. It produces enfeebled bodies, embittered minds and irritable spirits: thus it tells against good citizenship and good fellowship. Children are the most obvious sufferers, but those who have suffered in this way as children seldom come later to full strength or to physical and spiritual stability. It was found, when attempts were made to organize physical training classes for the unemployed, that most of these could not take advantage of the training offered; it made them too hungry.

Unemployment is the most hideous of our social evils, and has lately seemed to have become established in a peculiarly vicious form. We have long been acquainted with transitional, seasonal and cyclical unemployment—in which catalogue the adjectives represent a *crescendo* of evil; but now we have also to face long-term unemployment.

Transitional unemployment is no more than a period of inactivity between the completion of one job and the beginning of the next. With a reasonable scheme of Insurance it is no great evil, provided the period is short. It does not sap away a man's humanity.

Seasonal unemployment is necessarily incidental to some occupations in which, at certain seasons of the year, there is little work to be done. The seasons are known and it is possible to make provision for them. The Danes are the pioneers in this matter; it was part of the scheme of the People's High Schools that they would provide educational courses for periods of seasonal unemployment. The courses provided—in Danish history and literature and in the principles of co-operative farming—played a large part in securing for Denmark its high level of agricultural prosperity. By these and other devices, with a sound Insurance scheme, seasonal unemployment can be converted into valuable leisure.

Cyclical unemployment is a far more serious matter.[4] The history of trade, since the Industrial Revolution and the introduction of power-production, has shown alternating periods of prosperity and depression, 'boom' and 'slump'. Before 1914 a 'slump' caused suffering of appalling intensity; charitable people organized soup-kitchens and in other ways tried to save families from hunger and despair. The special problem caused by demobilization alike of soldiers and of munition-workers led to the establishment of what is unfairly called 'the dole', apart from which a revolution could hardly have been avoided. But still the volume of suffering caused by cyclical unemployment is fearful; for the period of inactivity is often long, so that the problem approximates to that of the worst form of the trouble, which is of comparatively recent origin and is now chronic.

This is long-term unemployment, which seems to be incurable under our present system except by the drastic remedy of war. For a study of this terrible social evil I must refer to *Men Without Work*, a survey financed by the Pilgrim Trust and published by the Cambridge University Press. The main points to notice are these:

(a) The worst evil of such unemployment, whether due to cyclical or to more permanent conditions, is its creating in the unemployed a sense that they have fallen out of the common life. However much their physical needs may be supplied (and before the war this supply was in many cases inadequate) the gravest part of the trouble remains; they are not wanted! That is the thing that has power to corrupt the soul of any man not already far advanced in saintliness. Because the man has no opportunity of service, he is turned upon himself and becomes, according to his temperament, a contented loafer or an embittered self-seeker. It has not been sufficiently appreciated that this moral isolation is the heaviest burden and most corrosive poison associated with unemployment: not bodily hunger but social futility. Consequently it is no remedy to pay the unemployed man as much as the employed; unless he has intellectual interests with which to occupy his leisure and is able to turn these into a means of service by study resulting in books or lectures, this will only make him content with idleness; and we have enough people suffering from that form of deadly sin (technically

called Sloth) at the other end of the social scale. Nothing will touch
the real need except to enable the man to do something which is
needed by the community. For it is part of the principle of
personality that we should live for one another.

(*b*) Much depends on the history and experience of the particular
individuals concerned. A recent enquiry disclosed the disquieting
fact that in a town where long-term unemployment was rife, the
older men, who had formerly had experience of full employment,
preferred to get back to work even at a wage less than their
unemployment benefit, while the younger, who had never had
regular emplyment, preferred to be idle 'on the dole' even if they
could earn a larger weekly sum. This does not mean that they were
happy in idleness; most of them were conscious of futility and
frustration (though they would not use those words about it), and
they were bitter against a world which had no use for them and
made no room for them; but they had a strong distaste for the
drudgery of regular work. They were degraded into a condition of
universal dissatisfaction.

The only real cure for unemployment is employment—beginning from the time when school-education is complete and
continuing, with no longer intervals than can be appreciated as
holidays, till strength begins to fail. In other words we are challenged to find a social order which provides employment, steadily
and generally, and our consciences should be restive till we succeed.
Christian sympathy demands this.

(2) What has been said about unemployment has already carried
us on to the second ground for the Church's concern in social
questions—the educational influence of the social and economic
system in which men live. This was first set forth by Plato in Books
VIII and IX of the *Republic*. The social order at once expresses the
sense of values active in the minds of citizens and tends to reproduce
the same sense of values in each new generation. If the State is so
ordered as to give great prominence to military leaders, as Sparta
was, as Prussia was, as Nazi Germany is, this must represent the
fact that the effective body of citizens, which may be a compact
minority, regards the military qualities as specially honourable or
specially important; and the system expressing that estimate

impresses it by perpetual suggestion upon every growing generation. So it is if wealth receives conspicuous honour.

The Nazis take all young Germans into the *Hitler-Jugend* and train them in the qualities admired and needed by the Nazi *régime*. We throw most young Englishmen out into a world of fierce competition where each has to stand on his own feet (which is good) and fight for his own interest (which is bad), if he is not to be submerged. Our system is not deliberately planned; but it produces effects just the same. It offers a perpetual suggestion in the direction of combative self-assertiveness. It is recognized on all hands that the economic system is an educative influence, for good or ill, of immense potency. Marshall, the prince of orthodox economists of the last generation, ranks it with the religion of a country as the most formative influence in the moulding of a people's character. If, so, then assuredly the Church must be concerned with it. For a primary concern of the Church is to develop in men a Christian character. When it finds by its side an educative influence so powerful it is bound to ask whether that influence is one tending to develop Christian character, and if the answer is partly or wholly negative the Church must do its utmost to secure a change in the economic system so that it may find in that system an ally and not an enemy. How far this is the situation in our country today we shall consider later. At present it is enough to say that the Church cannot, without betraying its own trust, omit criticism of the economic order, or fail to urge such action as may be prompted by that criticism.

(3) The existing system is challenged on moral grounds. It is not merely that some who 'have not' are jealous of some who 'have'. The charge against our social system is one of injustice. The banner so familiar in earlier unemployed or socialist processions—'Damn your charity; we want justice'—vividly exposes the situation as it was seen by its critics. If the present order is taken for granted or assumed to be sacrosanct, charity from the more or less foi ,unate would seem virtuous and commendable; to those for whom the order itself is suspect or worse, such charity is blood-money. Why should some be in the position to dispense and others to need that kind of charity?

An infidel could ignore that challenge, for apart from faith in God there is really nothing to be said for the notion of human equality. Men do not seem to be equal in any respect, if we judge by available evidence. But if all are children of one Father, then all are equal heirs of a status in comparison with which the apparent differences of quality and capacity are unimportant; in the deepest and most important of all—their relationship to God—all are equal. Why should some of God's children have full opportunity to develop their capacities in freely-chosen occupations, while others are confined to a stunted form of existence, enslaved to types of labour which represent no personal choice but the sole opportunity offered? The Christian cannot ignore a challenge in the name of justice. He must either refuse it or, accepting it, devote himself to removal of the stigma. The moral quality of the accusation brought against the economic and social order involves the Church in 'interference' on pain of betraying the trust committed to it.

(4) For the commission given to the Church is that it carry out the purpose of God. That is what is meant by the description of it as 'the Body of Christ'. It is to be the instrument or organ of His will, as His fleshly Body was in the days of His earthly ministry. That Body has many functions to fulfil, and one of them is suffering. The members of the Church do not, or should not, belong to it for what they can get in this world or in any other world; they—we—should belong to it in order to take our share in the great work, the fulfilment of God's purpose in the world and beyond it.

We know in outline what that is. God could make, and did make, multitudes of things which always obey His law for them—suns and planets, molecules and atoms, all that is studied in the 'natural sciences'. But He also made men and women, with hearts and wills that cannot be coerced but can respond freely, in order that they might be a fellowship of love answering the love with which He made them. But they used their freedom for self-seeking; so He came Himself to share our life and our death, in order that He might show that love which prompted the activity of creation in a form intelligible to men and women, the form of a human life. Thereby He gathered together a fellowship of those who respond to that appeal, to be at once the nucleus of the universal fellowship of love and the chief means to its establishment. (All this is a paraphrase of the Epistle to the Ephesians read from one angle. St. Paul is there wheeling round and round his theme, like an eagle in flight, and seeing it from many angles; but the theme is the purpose of God in creation, manifested in Jesus the Messiah, accomplished through the Church.)

If we belong to the Church with such a purpose and hope as this, we are obliged to ask concerning every field of human activity what is the purpose of God for it. If we find this purpose it will be the true and proper nature of that activity, and the relation of the various activities to one another in the divine purpose will be the 'Natural Order' of those activities. To bring them into that Order, if they have in fact departed from it, must be one part of the task of the Church as the Body of Christ. If what has true value as a means to an end beyond itself is in fact being sought as an end in itself, the Church must rebuke this dislocation of the structure of life and if possible point out the way of recovery. It is bound to 'interfere' because it is by vocation the agent of God's purpose, outside the scope of which no human interest or activity can fall.

# 2

## How should the Church Interfere?

When people talk about Church History they usually have in mind a record of theological controversies, General or other Councils, and the formulation of doctrines. All that is immensely important. But Church History is a vastly bigger thing than that; it is the story of the impact made by the Spirit of Christ upon the life of mankind.

The Church never gets credit for the greater part of what it does. That does not very much matter, because credit (like merit in Lord Melbourne's dictum) is 'only what one gentleman thinks of another gentleman'; and Christians are warned not to concern themselves about that.[1] No doubt some people would attend more to the Church and therefore also to its Gospel if they knew all that it really does in the world; that would be a gain as far as it goes; but each heart must know its need before it finds the satisfaction of that need in Christ. It is not so much to gain for the Church the credit and influence to which it is entitled that I emphasize the importance of clear thinking about the way in which the Church does its work, but rather for the avoidance of confusion of thought tending to calamitous results in practice.

Nine-tenths of the work of the Church in the world is done by Christian people fulfilling responsibilities and performing tasks which in themselves are not part of the official system of the Church at all. For example, the abolition of the Slave Trade and, later, of Slavery itself, was carried through by Wilberforce and his friends in the inspiration of their Christian faith and by means of appeal to the Christian principles professed by their fellow-citizens. The far-reaching reform of our penal system in the interval between the two wars has been effected by a group of men who, being concerned with its administration, thought out the question how, on Christian principles, a community ought to treat its own offenders. And apart from specific achievements like these there is the pervasive sweetening of life and of all human relationships by those who carry with them something of the Mind of Christ, received from Christian upbringing, from prayer and meditation, and from communion. No particular enterprises, nor all of them together, can compare in importance with the influence so exerted. To this extent they are justified who say that the task of the Church in face of social problems is to make good Christian men and women. That is by far its most important contribution. But (as I shall contend in a moment) it has others, less important and yet for their own purpose indispensable.

Next to the work of the Church done through its members in ordinary human relationships and in ordinary avocations, we may consider its work done through its members in their capacity as citizens shaping the political decisions which affect the national life and destiny. It is of crucial importance that the Church acting corporately should not commit itself to any particular policy. A policy always depends on technical decisions concerning the actual relations of cause and effect in the political and economic world; about these a Christian as such has no more reliable judgement than an atheist, except so far as he should be more immune to the temptations of self-interest. After the last war most Christian leaders in England strongly supported the principle of the League of Nations. The Bishop of Gloucester always dissented from this, and now holds that the League and its supporters are largely responsible for the outbreak of this present war, because they lured men to rely upon a security which in fact did not exist. It would be monstrous to suggest that this sincerely held judgement on the actual process of history proves him who holds it to be a less loyal or less whole-hearted Christian than the Bishops with whom he disagreed. The Church must not corporately be committed to either view. This refusal to adopt a particular policy is partly a matter of prudence, for the policy may turn out to be mistaken, as indeed every policy always turns out to have been less than perfectly adapted to the situation, and the Church must not be involved in its failure; still more is it a matter of justice, for even though a large majority of Christians hold a particular view, the dissentient minority may well be equally loyal to Christ and equally entitled to be recognized as loyal members of His Church. At the end of this book I shall offer, in my capacity as a Christian citizen, certain proposals for definite action which would, in my private judgement, conduce to a more Christian ordering of society; but if any member of the Convocation of York should be so ill-advised as to table a resolution that these proposals be adopted as a political programme for the Church, I should in my capacity as Archbishop resist that proposal with all my force, and should probably, as President of the Convocation, rule it out of order. The Church is committed to the everlasting Gospel and to the Creeds which formulate it; it must never commit itself to an ephemeral programme of detailed action.

But this repudiation of direct political action does not exhaust its political responsibility. It must explicitly call upon its members to exercise their citizenship in a Christian spirit. After the great Conference on Christian Politics, Economics and Citizenship (COPEC), held in Birmingham in 1924, the Christian ratepayers of a London Borough approached their Borough Council with a demand that their rates should be increased in order that some very bad housing in the Borough might be improved. When it became apparent, after the 'economic blizzard', that the Chancellor of the Exchequer would, for the first time in several years, have a surplus to dispose of, a great number of Christian income-tax payers wrote to their Members of Parliament to urge that restoration of the 'cuts' in unemployment relief should take precedence of any reduction in the rate of income-tax. There are frequently occasions when there is opportunity for general action in the political field; Christians should take advantage of these and ought to be able to feel that they have the support of the whole Church in doing so. To a considerable extent, though not by any means completely, the Conservative and Labour parties represent the 'haves' and the 'have-nots' respectively. That is politically unwholesome and ethically un-Christian. The Church must constantly press upon its members that the only question they should ask before casting their votes is the question—not What will best suit ME? but What will be best for the country?—and even then to take care that the standard of 'best' and 'worst' is the Christian standard. For it is tragically easy to be even fanatically devoted to a purely pagan ideal for one's nation; the Nazi movement has taught us that.

So far there is probably little dispute among Christians who have given serious thought to the subject. It is recognized that Christian men and women in the various walks of life should bring the spirit of Christ to bear upon their work, as well as on their purely personal relationships; and it is recognized, though perhaps not frequently enough asserted, that Christians should vote in a Christian spirit at least to the extent of preferring the public advantage to their own, and of subordinating the interest of their own section of society to that of a section evidently in greater need. But is this all? Is each individual Christian citizen to be left to work out by his own unaided effort what is the good of the community to which his own interest is to be subordinated? Can we, in face of the Nazi combination of complete personal self-dedication with absolute national egoism, still say it is no business of the Church to work out a scale of values for the political field?

I am to do what is best for my country? Very well. There is an opportunity to acquire for it additional wealth and power by merely expropriating some small State whose citizens are happy in their independence, or again by some successful diplomatic deception. Is it 'good' for my country to gain power or wealth by those means? Is it 'good' for a country to gain the whole world and to lose its own soul? If not, why not? Must there not be some ordered system of principles which represents the real 'good', and which is outraged by such conduct, however patriotic its motive or however successful its accomplishment?

It is here, as I contend, that the Church has to recover lost ground. It has in the past concerned itself very actively with these questions. It developed what was for the needs of the period a very complete system of principles by which those who were responsible for the public ordering of life might be guided. For a variety of reasons, at which we shall glance in the next chapter, this whole area of human activity was evacuated by the Church. Yet duties recognized as incumbent on the individual can scarecely be performed unless the Church recovers this lost territory.

In this enterprise we shall be censured for departure from our own contention that the Church is concerned with principles and not with policy. For the framing of policy knowledge of contemporary facts, and that power to estimate tendencies which comes only from specialist study, are indispensable. But a statement of principles will carry us on to ground commonly left during the last three centuries to purely secular forces; it is bound to seem like an intrusion into practical politics even when it scrupulously stops short. And the line of demarcation is not very clear. It may be possible to draw it with more definiteness when we have reviewed the history of the Church's enterprise or lack of it in this field, and have set out some of the principles concerned. The aim, however, is clear throughout. The Christian citizen is required in his civic action (e.g. voting) to promote the best interest of his country, with a Christian interpretation of the word 'best'; the aim of any formulation of Christian social principles is to provide that Christian interpretation or at least the means of reaching it.

So we answer the question 'How should the Church interfere?' by saying: In three ways—(1) its members must fulfil their moral responsibilities and functions in a Christian spirit; (2) its members must exercise their purely civil rights in a Christian spirit; (3) it must itself supply them with a systematic statement of principles to aid them in doing these two things, and this will carry with it a denunciation of customs or institutions in contemporary life and practice which offend against those principles.

There remains the question whether or not the Church should ever interfere in a particular issue, such as, for example, an actual trade dispute which has broken out. It can be answered with almost complete assurance that the Church, acting officially, should stand aside. It has its own witness to give; and if this were needed, no dispute would arise. It is very seldom that Christianity offers a solution of practical problems; what it can do is to lift the parties to a level of thought and feeling at which the problem disappears. In parts of south-eastern Europe there are regions in which different races and cultures are so intermingled that there is no hope of establishing justice among them so long as each asserts its claim against the other. So long as that condition exists, the problem to which it gives rise is insoluble. If, on the other hand, all could be brought to love their neighbours as themselves, there would be no problem. It would not be solved; it would be abolished.

So it was that our Lord refused to settle a dispute about an inheritance. One of two brothers had a grievance; he thought he was not getting the share due to him; so he came with the request: 'Master, bid my brother divide the inheritance with me.' But He refused to settle the dispute—'Man, who made Me a judge or a divider over you?' Instead, He tells them how to avoid having a dispute to settle: 'Take heed, and keep yourselves from all covetousness.'[2] For, of course, if there had been no covetousness in either brother, there would have been no dispute.

But though the Church, and its agents acting in its name, cannot undertake to give judgement between contending parties, they may, as promoters of goodwill, try to bring the contending parties together. So Bishop Westcott secured a settlement of a Durham coal-strike by pleading with each side to recognize what was fair in the contention of the other, till they came in fact to an agreement. No one questions the propriety of the Bishop's action in that case. Let me illustrate the principle further by reference to the action of a group of Bishops, of whom I was one, in 1926—the action which led to Lord Baldwin's comment quoted near the beginning of this book. The coal-strike, which had been the occasion of the general strike, had lasted several months. These Bishops decided to try to bring the parties together. They had no proposals of their own to make—that would have been to go beyond their province. But there had been a Royal Commission and its recommendations had not been adopted. We decided to see how far the representatives of the Coal-Owners and the representatives of the Miners would be willing to come towards agreement in acceptance of those recommendations. Both parties were willing to meet us. At that date the Miners were ready to accept the proposals of the Commission as a basis of negotiation; the Owners were not. But as the Owners had at first been willing to do so if the Miners would do so as well, it seemed right to report to the Prime Minister what we had found. Our effort was a failure. It is arguable that nothing but success (such as Bishop Westcott achieved) justifies any intervention. My plea is that it could hardly ever be right for the Church or ecclesiastical persons as such to propose terms for the solution of a dispute, because they lack the specialist knowledge required; it is certainly right for them to urge the spirit and method of conciliation; and it very well may be right for them to recall the parties to proposals made by competent persons, such as a Royal Commission appointed for the purpose, with a view to seeing whether or not these may supply the basis for a solution.

Yet even if such action is occasionally justified, the main task of the Church must be to inculcate Christian principles and the power of the Christian spirit.

# 3

## *Has the Church Claimed to Intervene Before?*

It is often suggested that the claim advanced in the last chapter is a novel one, and that in making it the Church is straying outside its traditional and proper province. No doubt in the eighteenth century the Church did confine itself almost entirely to theology and piety. At all times these are fundamental. Unless the Church has something to stand for, it has no place of its own in the ordering of life, and becomes merely a group of people who like or value their association with one another. All special character in the Church comes from its Dogma—the divinely given truth which it believes itself commissioned to proclaim; this is worked out in its theology; so it is always necessary that dogma and theology should be the basis of the Church's life. Further, no effect can be produced unless individuals genuinely respond to this; and this response is faith and piety. So what happened in the eighteenth century was a retirement, so to speak, upon the central citadel. Wearied with the controversies of the sixteenth century, distraught by the religious wars of the seventeenth (of which our Civil War was one), men fell back in their religious life upon what is most central and fundamental. The spirit of man needed to recuperate; but having regained freshness it sallied forth again, under the inspiration of its central faith, in the Methodist movement, the Tractarian revival and the Christian social enterprise.

Such recoveries always seem like sheer innovations to those who are ignorant of History. To us it seems natural and proper that religion should control personal conduct alike in its most open and in its most intimate aspects; we have already seen what Lord Melbourne thought about that claim to control private life; many feel much the same about its determination to interfere with the affairs of public life. But this, too, is nothing new. From the very outset Christian faith has intimately affected social as well as personal conduct, and the main Christian tradition carries with it a massive body of social teaching.

The primitive Church expressed its intimacy of inner fellowship by a spontaneous community of goods. It was a small fellowship of persons filled with the spirit of Christ and therefore with love for one another. This expressed itself in a voluntary communism. But the whole character and merit of this lay in its being voluntary. The disciples had possessions, but did not reckon them as their own. This could not have lasted. Even if the purity of the Church had been maintained, its extension would have led to complications. Yet the primitive community supplies the norm and standard. It is as different from what is ordinarily called communism as anything can be; it is, indeed, its polar opposite. Modern communism abolishes legal ownership by private persons; under it no one has property to give away. What St. Peter said to Ananias shows that the primitive Church recognized legal ownership and laid on its members no compulsion to forgo this.[1] He and his wife Sapphira had followed the general movement up to a point; they sold their land, and gave part of the price to the common fund, keeping back another part. But they pretended that they were giving the whole, and that pretence, not the retention of part of the property, was their crime. 'Why hath Satan filled thy heart to lie to the Holy Spirit and to keep back part of the price of the land? Whilst it remained, did it not remain thine own? And after it was sold, was it not in thy power?'

This is a point of vital importance. Psychologically and morally there is all the difference in the world between voluntary and compulsory poverty, between a free sharing of goods and a compulsory abolition of personal ownership. Psychologically it is a fact that the spirit of adventure can only thrive on a basis of security; morally, sacrifice is only possible where possession is admitted. To renounce property is a conspicuously vivid act of personal freedom; to have no property or to be forcibly deprived of it is a serious infringement of personal freedom.

What now concerns us, however, is that from the very outset Christian faith found for itself social and economic expression. It did not at that stage take the form of a set of principles for the guidance of the State: the primitive Church was a handful of people quite unable to influence the Jewish State, let alone the Roman Empire. But as the Church grew it began to develop its own social philosophy. It could not fail to be influenced by the Mosaic legislation, such as the Law of Jubilee (Leviticus 25) which is a piece of land-legislation of immense significance, and the prohibition of usury (Leviticus 25 and Deuteronomy 23). The growth of the Church led to the need for a statement of social principles for the guidance of its own members while they were a considerable though unrecognized and often persecuted minority, and later, when the Church was recognized and became a factor of influence in public life, for the guidance of the State.

The fundamental Biblical principle is that the earth—land—belongs to God; men enjoy the use of it, and this use may be so regulated as to ensure to particular families both security in that enjoyment and exclusive right to it. But this was to be so done as to ensure also that all members of the community shared in the enjoyment of some portion. There was to be no proletariat. There were thus to be rights of property, but they were rights shared by all, and were subject to the overruling consideration that God alone had ultimate ownership of the land, the families to whom it was allotted being His stewards. The Law of Jubilee, by which every fifty years alienated land reverted to its proper family, so that the permanent accumulation of a large estate in a single hand became impossible, rested on this basic principle of divine ownership. In the days of the Kings we find prophets denouncing such accumulations; so for example Isaiah exclaims: 'Woe unto them that join house to house, that lay field to field, till there be no room and yet be made to dwell alone in the midst of the land' (Isaiah 5.8); and Micah: 'Woe to them that devise iniquity and work evil upon their beds! When the morning is light, they practise it, because it is in the power of their hand. And they covet fields and seize them;

and houses, and take them away; and they oppress a man and his house, even a man and his heritage' (Micah 2.1, 2). And the evil here was not primarily economic though that may have been involved. The evil was the denial of what Tertullian (c. 160–230) would call 'fellowship in property'—which seemed to him the natural result of unity in mind and spirit.

Of course the Mosaic legislation was designed for a community dependent on its own land. We are not; today there is a world-community in economic matters though not yet in political matters. But in any case it is for principles and not for precepts that Christians turn to the Old Testament.

The position which the Church reached before the conversion of Constantine (312) brought fuller responsibilities is most plainly stated by Lactantius. His basic conceptions are equality in the enjoyment of God's bounty and (by consequence) the justice of a claim put forward by the needy to share with those who have more than a sufficiency. He is still writing for a Christian minority in the State, where unity of heart and mind, with general goodwill, is presumed.

The institution of property is regarded as rooted in sin; for if all men loved God with all their hearts and their neighbours as themselves, they would cheerfully labour for the common good and would take for themselves no more than their fair share. But men are sinful, so property-rights are needed, not so much for the satisfaction of the rich as for the protection of the poor.

When we pass to the next period, in which Christians were not only recognized but counted the Emperor among their number, we find a changed emphasis. They are carrying a new responsibility. They have lost much in intimacy of fellowship among themselves and all that springs from this; they have gained in the power, and therefore the duty, to influence the State. St. Ambrose (340–397) was a great officer of State as well as a Bishop. He lays it down that 'nature produced all things for the common use of all men, and that nature produced the common right of property, but usurpation the private right; or again that God wished the earth to be the common possession of all men, to produce its fruits for all men, but avarice created the rights of property.'[2]

Yet this was not a foundation for Communism. It did, indeed, mean that if men were morally perfect—that is, altogether guided by justice and love—there would be no private property. But men are not like that, and in the world as it is the Fathers hold that private property is a legitimate institution. It cannot claim the dignity of being a direct expression of the Divine Will; but it is an expression of that Will in the conditions resulting from men's failure to fulfil the Divine intention. Consequently there are from the outset limitations upon the rights of property. It is, for example, instructive and important that St. Ambrose regards almsgiving as an act of justice rather than of mercy.

St. Augustine taught explicitly that private property is the creation of the State and exists only in virtue of the State's protection. But the State, according to him, has its origin in the sinfulness of men, which must be kept within bounds. So the State has a divine authority, yet was instituted only because of men's sin. This position is the same as that of St. Ambrose, but rooted a little further back in social philosophy. Gratian, who made the great compilation of Canon Law in the twelfth century, takes this same position. Private property is lawful as an accommodation to man's sinful state.

In all these writers the influence of Stoic teaching can be traced. When we come to the completest medieval statement—in St. Thomas Aquinas—this influence is reinforced by that of Aristotle. Consequently St. Thomas bases the State on the essentially social nature of man. Consonantly with this he draws a distinction between property as a right of administration and distribution (*potestas procurandi et dispensandi*) which he holds to be lawful, and property as a right to exclusive use, which he holds to be unlawful.[5]

His defence of the first is interestingly modern. Property of this sort is, he says, 'necessary to human life for three reasons. First, because every man is more careful in administering what belongs to himself alone than that which is common to many or to all; since each one would shirk the labour and leave to another that which is the business of everybody, as happens where there is a multitude of servants. Secondly, because human affairs are conducted in more orderly fashion if each man is charged with taking care of some particular thing himself, whereas there would be confusion if every one were looking after everything indiscriminately. Thirdly, because a more peaceful state is ensured to man if each one is contented with his own. Hence it is to be observed that quarrels arise more frequently among those who possess something in common and without division.'

But with regard to use or enjoyment St. Thomas says that man ought not to possess external things as private but as common, so that he readily shares them with others in their need. So clear is this to him, as to Lactantius and Ambrose, that he expressly declared 'theft' to be no sin if it is committed to relieve genuine need. Of course the need must be real and urgent, and other means of meeting it lacking; but then 'it is lawful for a man to succour his own need by means of another's property, by taking it either openly or secretly; nor is this properly speaking theft or robbery.'[4]

It is thus evident that it is part of the common Christian tradition from primitive times to the fullest development of medieval thought that Christian faith should find expression in relation to economic questions. It is further evident that in this tradition the rights of property, while perfectly legitimate, are always an accommodation to human sin, are subordinate to the general interest, and are a form of stewardship rather than of ultimate ownership.

In its whole social teaching, the Church stood on a firm Biblical foundation. The Reformers repudiated large parts of the tradition in the desire to return from ecclesiastical to Biblical authority; but in fact their position was in this respect less fully Biblical than that of the medieval Church. They found their justification of property in the Eighth Commandment, on the ground that a divine prohibition of theft presupposes a divine sanction of property. So, of course, it does. But the Puritan simplification of religious teaching, which in this field took the form of an exclusive emphasis on the Decalogue, had the effect of breaking up a tradition derived from Biblical teaching as a whole. That teaching certainly included the reality and rightfulness of private property; but it also contained provisions which made the actual rights of property conditional rather than absolute.

Yet the Reformers by no means exempted ownership from moral responsibilities, and so influential a Puritan writer as Ames still held the view that 'all things become common in extreme necessity'. Baxter, however, inclines to the view that the prohibition of theft is absolute, without enquiring what—morally—constitutes theft.

The Reformers on the Continent and the Puritans in England were dealing with a new situation. There was a fresh and deepened sense of individual responsibility which they regarded as spiritually sound, and of which they became the prophets. All that heightened this they welcomed, and among the rest they welcomed the free right to acquire and dispose of property. They taught a high standard as regards the spending of it, and for the first time made the keeping of accounts a religious duty. The more conservative of the Reformers were forced to define their position over against the extremer reforming sects, so that among the Thirty-nine Articles of Religion, one, the thirty-eighth, declared that 'the Riches and Goods of Christians are not common as touching the right, title and possession of the same, as certain Anabaptists do falsely boast'. Thus, even where the Reformers agreed with the medieval theologians, as they very largely did, their emphasis tended to shift from the communal restrictions upon private property to its exclusive rights and its moral responsibilities. Profitable industry was presented as a duty; so was careful spending, thrifty provision for the future, and charity to the poor. Wesley was true to this tradition in his three-fold exhortation, 'Gain all you can; save all you can; give all you can.' He was very thorough about the second and third. He denounced the notion that an increased income justifies an increased personal expenditure. 'Perhaps you say you can now *afford* the expense. This is the quintessence of nonsense. Who gave you this addition to your fortune, or (to speak properly) who *lent* it to you? To speak more properly still, who lodged it for a time in your hands as His steward? . . . This *Affording* to rob God is the very cant of hell.'[5]

Such a declaration by the founder of Methodism in the eighteenth century carries us back to the fourteenth, in which a Schoolman wrote: 'He who has enough to satisfy his wants and nevertheless ceaselessly labours to acquire riches, either in order to obtain a higher social position, or that subsequently he may have enough to live without labour, or that his sons may become men of wealth and importance—all such are incited by damnable avarice, sensuality and pride.'[6] But no Schoolman could have said, 'Gain all you can,' and it is hard to fit such an injunction into the New Testament, which regards riches, not indeed as an actual evil, but as a snare. Apart from this the actual conduct demanded by Schoolmen and Reformers was not very different. But the Reformers made changes in the foundations which affected the whole structure. The two main pillars of medieval theological economics were the doctrine of the Just Price and the Prohibition of Usury.

With the intricacies of the Just Price we are not now concerned. What is important for our argument is the fact that this principle was stated as part of a complete theology. Its interpretation and application to practice varied from one century to another, partly as circumstances altered, partly as men gained a fuller insight into the economic process. The principle itself is clear—that the price of an article should be fixed on moral grounds with due regard to cost of material and labour and to reasonable profit; the vendor is not entitled merely to ask the utmost that the purchaser will pay. Above all, he must on no account charge more because the buyer's need is great. The fullest statement of it was worked out by St. Antonino of Florence in the fifteenth century; he recognized the actual pressures of the market and allowed much elasticity in application of the principle; but the principle stood firm—there is a price which it is reasonable and right to charge, and to take more, however willing purchasers may be to pay, is avarice. We find this still held by the early Calvinists, but the relaxation of the ban on usury led to the collapse of the whole system. At this point there was what looked like a sharp reversal of doctrine. To this vital but far from simple topic we now turn.

The Mosaic Law forbade usury. But (1) what was chiefly in mind in that primitive community was the exploitation of the needy; 'the lending of business capital on terms offering good chances of repayment was not in question';[7] (2) the Mosaic prohibition of usury only affects loans to a brother-Israelite; within Israel the prohibition was absolute, but between an Israelite and a Gentile it was permitted.[8] (Incidentally, it was this last consideration, coupled with the prohibition of usury to Christians and the exclusion of Jews from many occupations, which turned the Jews into the moneylenders of Europe.)

Now the Church was always in difficulties about this prohibition. What it was quite clear about was the sinfulness of avarice. In the conditions of any period before about 1300 A.D. a suitable rough and ready test was to ask whether the principal was safe; if it was, interest ought not to be charged. To share profits as partners in an enterprise was legitimate; to share profits where risks also had to be shared was legitimate. But to make barren money breed by merely lending it at interest without risk of its loss was not legitimate. The system of debentures is of all things the most opposed to earlier medieval teaching.

This reflects the circumstances of the time rather than any permanent principle. The theories of value varied as the centuries passed, and St. Antonino of Florence represents a half-way stage between St. Thomas and Calvin.

Luther, a peasant, was conservative in politics and in social ethics. He condemned the practice of all usury as loudly as any Schoolman. Calvin was a townsman, vividly aware of the economic virtues. He did not hold that to get rich was proof of wickedness; he did not condemn the accumulation of riches, but only the use of them for indulgence or ostentation. His condonation of usury is indeed most cautiously hedged about so as to exclude all exploitation of real need; it was said of him that 'Calvin deals with usurie as the apothecarie doth with poison'. But that he was ready to deal with it at all was the decisive matter. He set the door ajar; the pressure of economic progress would throw it wide open, unless principles for its regulation were worked out to take the place of the discarded principle of prohibition. But in the turmoil of those turbulent times this was never done. So Calvin had unwittingly opened the way for the coming of Economic Man.

That was not Calvin's intention, and the practice of early Calvinists shows that they had no toleration for 'get-rich-quick' devices, as we may see from the records of the Pilgrim Fathers and early history of Massachusetts.

'Consider the case of Mr. Robert Keane. His offence, by general consent, was black. He kept a shop in Boston, in which he took "in some . . . above 6d. in the shilling profit; in some above 8d.; and in some small things above two for one"; and this, though he was "an ancient professor of the gospel, a man of eminent parts, wealthy and having but one child, having come over for conscience' sake and for the advancement of the gospel." The scandal was terrible. Profiteers were unpopular—"the cry of the country was great against oppression"—and the grave elder reflected that a reputation for greed would injure the infant community, lying as it did "under the curious observation of all Churches and civil States in the world." In spite of all, the magistrates were disposed to be lenient. There was no positive law in force limiting profits; it was not easy to determine what profits were fair; the sin of charging what the market could stand was not peculiar to Mr. Keane; and, after all, the law of God required no more than double restitution. So they treated him mercifully, and fined him only £200.'[9]

None the less, the door was ajar, and the pressure of life would open it so widely that Calvinism, which began as a system of regimentation, where economic activity was subject to severe moral restraint, became ultimately the mainspring of unrestricted enterprise and competition. Its profound and essential individualism overthrew its relatively superficial authoritarianism. This process had already gone far by the date of the English Civil War. Archbishop Laud owed much of his unpopularity with the section of society then represented in Parliament to his vigorous action, often high-handed, in checking the robbery of the poor by the encroachment of landlords and the 'enclosing' of common lands. He stood for the older ethics of a peasant civilization. The Puritans had their strength in the towns with their expanding business enterprise, among whom 'Gain all you can' was a commendable precept even when 'Give all you can', which alone can justify it, was honoured more than it was obeyed.

The Reformers never intended to produce such a monster as the Economic Man of the last hundred and fifty years; the Puritans were austere in their demands for self-denial in respect of most things which money can buy. But their fundamental individualism, which brought a fuller sense of personal responsibility to God, also at the same time undermined the appreciation of wealth as essentially social and therefore subject at all points to control in the interest of society as a whole.

Consequently, when the great opportunities for making wealth arrived there was much religious teaching to encourage enterprise in that direction, and no accepted traditional body of doctrine to relate the new enterprise to the old faith. This goes far to account for the paralysis of the Church in face of the Industrial Revolution. First in iron works, then in spinning and weaving, the new industry was developed—very largely by adherents of Puritanism. As the fierce energy of their faith in God declined, there was nothing left to restrain the competition for wealth, while there was a moral deposit of approbation for its accumulation. Karl Marx is not far wrong in his famous declaration that '*the bourgeoise*, wherever it got the upper hand, put an end to all feudal, patriarchal, idyllic relations, pitilessly tore asunder the motley feudal ties that bound man to his "natural superiors", and left remaining no other bond between man and man than naked self-interest and callous cash payment.'[10]

There was nearly a century during which the social witness of the Church was almost unheard. There were splendid parish priests who fought for the people's rights—men like Comber, who was Rector of Kirkby Moorside from 1760 to 1810, and resisted the Enclosure Acts, founded schools, and in a variety of practical ways stood up for the oppressed. Greatest of all was Hook, Vicar of Leeds from 1837 to 1859, who both set the type or ideal for the modern Town Parson and steadily championed the cause of the common people. But these were individual stalwarts, mainly concentrating attention on particular evils. For the revival of Christian social doctrine we have to wait till Ludlow, Maurice and Kingsley take the field. From their time onwards the recovery has been steady. It would be tedious to recount the deliverances of official Church bodies which reflect the influence of those prophets and, in a later generation, of Westcott, Gore, and Scott Holland—whose names bring us down to living and contemporary problems.

Enough has been said to show that there is an authentic tradition of Christian social teaching. But like other parts of the Christian tradition, it is a living thing, proving its vitality in the only way in which that can be done by showing a capacity to relate itself effectively to changing conditions and circumstances. Accordingly our own presentation will not begin with ancient authorities but with a statement of first principles.

# 4

## Christian Social Principles:

### (A) PRIMARY

The method of the Church's impact upon society at large should be twofold. The Church must announce Christian principles and point out where the existing social order at any time is in conflict with them. It must then pass on to Christian citizens, acting in their civic capacity, the task of re-shaping the existing order in closer conformity to the principles. For at this point technical knowledge may be required and judgements of practical expediency are always required. If a bridge is to be built, the Church may remind the engineer that it is his obligation to provide a really safe bridge; but it is not entitled to tell him whether, in fact, his design meets this requirement; a particular theologian may also be a competent engineer, and, if he is, his judgement on this point is entitled to attention; but this is altogether because he is a competent engineer and his theological equipment has nothing whatever to do with it. In just the same way the Church may tell the politician what ends the social order should promote; but it must leave to the politician the devising of the precise means to those ends.

This is a point of first-rate importance, and is frequently misunderstood. If Christianity is true at all it is a truth of universal application; all things should be done in the Christian spirit and in accordance with Christian principles. 'Then,' say some, 'produce your Christian solution of unemployment.' But there neither is nor could be such a thing. Christian faith does not by itself enable its adherent to foresee how a vast multitude of people, each one partly selfish and partly generous, and an intricate economic mechanism, will in fact be affected by a particular economic or political innovation—'social credit', for example. 'In that case,' says the reformer—or, quite equally, the upholder of the *status quo*—'keep off the turf. By your own confession you are out of place here.' But this time the Church must say 'No; I cannot tell you what is the remedy; but I can tell you that a society of which unemployment (in peace time) is a chronic feature is a diseased society, and that if you are not doing all you can to find and administer the remedy, you are guilty before God.' Sometimes the Church can go further than this and point to features in the social structure itself which are bound to be sources of social evil because they contradict the principles of the Gospel.

So the Church is likely to be attacked from both sides if it does its duty. It will be told that it has become 'political' when in fact it has been careful only to state principles and point to breaches of them; and it will be told by advocates of particular policies that it is futile because it does not support these. If it is faithful to its commission it will ignore both sets of complaints, and continue so far as it can to influence all citizens and permeate all parties.

Before going on to state in outline the chief principles of Christian social doctrine, it may be wise, in the prevailing temper of our age, to add a further word of caution. For it is sometimes supposed that what the Church has to do is to sketch a perfect social order and urge men to establish it. But it is very difficult to know what a 'perfect social order' means. Is it the order that would work best if we were all perfect? Or is it the order that would work best in a world of men and women such as we actually are? If it is the former, it certainly ought not to be established; we should wreck it in a fortnight. If it is the latter, there is no reason for expecting the Church to know what it is.

Here we are dealing with what is at this moment the least popular part of traditional Christianity: the doctrine of Original Sin. No doubt this has often been put forward in ways which men today find peculiar difficulty in accepting. It would be quite out of place to deal with the whole topic here. Quite enough for our present purpose may be expressed as follows. When we open our eyes as babies we see the world stretching out around us; we are in the middle of it; all proportions and perspectives in what we see are determined by the relation—distance, height, and so forth—of the various visible objects to ourselves. This will remain true of our bodily vision as long as we live. I am the centre of the world I see; where the horizon is depends on where I stand. Now just the same thing is true at first of our mental and spiritual vision. Some things hurt us; we hope they will not happen again; we call them bad. Some things please us; we hope they will happen again; we call them good. Our standard of value is the way things affect ourselves. So each of us takes his place in the centre of his own world. But I am not the centre of the world, or the standard of reference as between good and bad; I am not, and God is. In other words, from the beginning I put myself in God's place. This is my original sin. I was doing it before I could speak, and everyone else has been doing it from early infancy. I am not 'guilty' on this account because I could not help it. But I am in a state, from birth, in which I shall bring disaster on myself and everyone affected by my conduct unless I can escape from it. Education may make my self-centredness less disastrous by widening my horizon of interest; so far it is like the climbing of a tower, which widens the horizon for physical vision while leaving me still the centre and standard of reference. Education may do more than this if it succeeds in winning me into devotion to truth or to beauty; that devotion may effect a partial deliverance from self-centredness. But complete deliverance can be effected only by the winning of my whole heart's devotion, the total allegiance of my will—and this only the Divine Love disclosed by Christ in His Life and Death can do.[1]

The political problem is concerned with men as they are, not with men as they ought to be. Part of the task is so to order life as to lead them nearer to what they ought to be; but to assume that they are already this will involve certain failure and disaster. It is not contended that men are utterly bad, nor that they are more bad than good. What is contended is that they are not perfectly good, and that even their goodness is infected with a quality—self-centredness—which partly vitiates it, and exposes them to temptations so far as they achieve either freedom or power. This does not mean that freedom or power should be denied to them; on the contrary, it is fundamental to the Christian position that men should have freedom even though they abuse it; but it is also to be recognized that they certainly will abuse it except so far as they are won by devotion to truth or to beauty to that selfless outlook, which is only perfectly established in men by love which arises in them in answer to the redemptive love of God.

In any period worth considering, and probably to the end of earthly history, statesmen will themselves be men, and will be dealing with men, who abuse feedom and power. Now the most fundamental requirement of any political and economic system is not that it shall express love, though that is desirable, nor that it shall express justice, though that is the first ethical demand to be made upon it, but that it shall supply some reasonable measure of security against murder, robbery and starvation. If it can be said with real probability that a proposed scheme would in fact, men being what they are, fail to provide that security, that scheme is doomed. Christians have some clues to the understanding of human nature which may enable them to make a more accurate estimate than others of these points. But they will not, if they are true to their own tradition, approach the question with rosy-tinted spectacles. Its assertion of Original Sin should make the Church intensely realistic, and conspicuously free from Utopianism.

There is no such thing as a Christian social ideal, to which we should conform our actual society as closely as possible. We may notice, incidentally, about any such ideals from Plato's *Republic* onwards, that no one really wants to live in the ideal state as depicted by anyone else. Moreover, there is the desperate difficulty of getting there. When I read any description of an Ideal State and think how we are to begin transforming our own society into that, I am reminded of the Englishman in Ireland who asked the way to Roscommon. 'Is it Roscommon you want to go to?' asked the Irishman. 'Yes,' said the Englishman; 'that's why I asked the way.' 'Well,' said the Irishman, 'if I wanted to go to Roscommon, I wouldn't be starting from here.'

But though Christianity supplies no ideal in this sense, it supplies something of far more value—namely, principles on which we can begin to act in every possible situation. To the consideration of these we now turn.

## 1. *God and His Purpose*

All Christian thinking, and Christian thinking about society no less than any other, must begin not with man but with God. The fundamental conviction is that God is the creator of the world which could not begin or continue except by His will. The world is not necessary to God in the sense in which God is necessary to the world; for if there were no God, there would be no world; but if there were no world, God would be just what He is—only (presumably) about to make the world. For He is impelled to make the world by His love; as Plato saw, He is far removed from envy and wishes to share out His blessedness. The world is not necessary to God as the object of His love, for He has that within Himself in the relation of the Persons of the Blessed Trinity; but it results from His love; creation is a kind of overflow of the divine love. In making the world He brought into existence vast numbers of things which always have to obey His law for them—from stars and planets to atoms and electrons; these have no choice but to obey. But He also made creatures—men and women—who could disobey His law for them, and do so; He did this in order that among His creatures there might be some who gave Him a free obedience and answered His love with theirs. This involved the risk, amounting to a moral certainty, that they would take the self-centred outlook upon life, and then, partly by imitation and partly in self-defence, become hardened in selfishness, till society was a welter of competing selfishness instead of being a fellowship of love. That is what happened. To win them out of this, He came on earth and lived out the divine love in a human life and death. He is increasingly drawing men to Himself by the love thus shown. Lord Acton, who knew more history than any other Englishman of the last generation, deliberately declared: 'The action of Christ who is risen on mankind whom He redeemed fails not, but increases'.[2] But this task of drawing all men to Himself, the divine purpose to 'sum up all things in Christ',[3] will not be effected till the end of history, and the fellowship of love which it is the divine plan to establish cannot come into being in its completeness within history at all, for it must be more than a fellowship of contemporaries. The Kingdom of God is a reality here and now, but can be perfect only in the eternal order.

### 2. *Man: his Dignity, Tragedy and Destiny*

The fundamental facts about man are two: he is made 'in the image of God'; and this image is, so to speak, stamped upon an animal nature. Between these two there is constant tension resulting in perpetual tragedy.

The dignity of man is that he is the child of God, capable of communion with God, the object of the Love of God—such love as is displayed on the Cross—and destined for eternal fellowship with God. His true value is not what he is worth in himself or to his earthly state, but what he is worth to God; and that worth is bestowed on Him by the utterly gratuitous Love of God.

All his life should be conducted and ordered with this dignity in view. The State must not treat him as having value only so far as he serves its ends, as Totalitarian States do; the State exists for its citizens, not the citizens for the State. But neither must a man treat himself, or conduct his life, as if he were himself the centre of his own value; he is not his own end; his value is his worth to God and his end is 'to glorify God and enjoy Him for ever.'

As a child of God, man is a member of a family, the family of God. This in complete development and expression is nothing less than mankind. But the inherently social and indeed 'familial' character of man finds its first expression in the human family. This is the initial form of man's social life, and its preservation and security is the first principle of social welfare. On one side the family is a biological fact; children are born utterly dependent and need the care of both parents. But it is far more than biological. Other animals care for their young; but when the young are mature, the family connexion ceases. Among human beings the family tie lasts through life; what begins as a biological necessity becomes a spiritual possession. To ignore the family, as much in the organization of contemporary life ignores it, is to injure both citizens and society.

There are wider social units which are also necessary; with some of these we shall be concerned later, but only one is natural in a way at all resembling that in which the family is natural—and then in markedly less degree. The nation as we know it is a product of long history; but its origins in the clan and the tribe give it the same relation as the family to the individual. And it is a product of historical development, not a deliberately manufactured structure. Every civilized man or woman is born a member of a nation as well as of a family. These nations have developed various cultural types, and the world is the richer for that variety.

Each individual is born into a family and a nation. In his maturity he is very largely what these have made him. The family is so deeply grounded in nature and the nation in history that anyone who believes in God as Creator and as Providence is bound to regard both as part of the divine plan for human life. Their claims have to be adjusted to one another, and so have the claims of the several families within each nation and of the several nations in the family of mankind. But any ordering of society which impairs or destroys the stability of the family stands condemned on that account alone; and any ordering of international life which obliterates the freedom of the several nations to develop their own cultural traditions is also condemned. The aim within the nation must be to create a harmony of stable and economically secure family units; the aim in the world as a whole must be to create a harmony of spiritually independent nations which recognize one another as reciprocally supplementary parts of a richly harmonious fellowship.

Such a harmony would be the earthly counterpart and 'first fruits' (as St. Paul might call it) of the perfected Kingdom of God. It would supply the school, training the citizens of that Kingdom—of which the full life cannot be known under earthly conditions, for it is a fellowship of the servants of God in all generations alike with Him and with one another.

It is the tragedy of man that he conceives such a state of affairs and knows it for the only satisfaction of his nature, yet so conducts his life as to frustrate all hope of attaining that satisfaction. It is not only that his spirit and reason have as yet established but little control over the animal part of his nature; it is his spirit which is depraved, his reason which is perverted. His self-centredness infects his idealism because it distorts all his perspectives. So far as his reason acts in purely intellectual ways it may be trustworthy: $2 + 2 = 4$; that really is true; it is not the best approximation that can be expected of sinful man; it is an exact apprehension of absolute truth. Within what is capable of mathematical treatment man has this grasp of truth. But it carries us only a little way. It helps us to make and manipulate aeroplanes; it does not help us to use them always and only for the benefit of mankind. All science is morally neutral. When we come to human relationships, to friendship, to falling in love—and out of it again—to social organization or to political construction, we enter on a sphere of life where reason is very fallible. Self-interest is always exercising its disturbing influence, not less (though more nobly) when it is being forcibly repudiated than when it is accepted as the guide of conduct.

Anyhow, we all know that Politics is largely a contention between different groups of self-interest—e.g. the Haves and the Have-nots. It may be the function of the Church to lead people to a purely disinterested virtue (though this is at least debatable); a statesman who supposes that a mass of citizens can be governed without appeal to their self-interest is living in dreamland and is a public menace. The art of government in fact is the art of so ordering life that self-interest prompts what justice demands. Thus it is enacted that thieves should be sent to prison; but the object of the law is not to imprison thieves, but to make men reflect that even if they are not honest they are still prudent to behave honestly.

Yet these expedients are not purely prudential, and though the cynic finds plenty of material for his malicious wit, the real truth about man eludes his grasp. Man is self-centred; but he always carries with him abundant proof that this is not the real truth of his nature. He has to his credit both capacities and achievements that could never be derived from self-interest. The image of God—the image of holiness and love—is still there, though defaced; it is the source of his aspirations; it is even—through its defacement—the occasion of his perversity. It is capable of response to the Divine Image in its perfection if ever this can be presented to it. This is the glory of the Gospel. It enables man to see 'the light of the knowledge of the glory of God in the face of Jesus Christ', and so 'with unveiled face, reflecting as a mirror the glory of the Lord', man may be 'transformed into the same image from glory to glory.'[4]

That is man's destiny. And his social life, so far as it is deliberately planned, should be ordered with that destiny in view. He must be treated as what he actually is, but always with a view to what in God's purpose he is destined to become. For the law, and the social order, is our schoolmaster to bring us to Christ.[5]

# 5

## Christian Social Principles:

### (B)   DERIVATIVE

#### 1.   *Freedom*

The primary principle of Christian Ethics and Christian Politics must be respect for every person simply as a person. If each man and woman is a child of God, whom God loves and for whom Christ died, then there is in each a worth absolutely independent of all usefulness to society. The person is primary, not the society; the State exists for the citizen, not the citizen for the State. The first aim of social progress must be to give the fullest possible scope for the exercise of all powers and qualities which are distinctly personal; and of these the most fundamental is deliberate choice.

Consequently society must be so arranged as to give to every citizen the maximum opportunity for making deliberate choices and the best possible training for the use of that opportunity. In other words, one of our first considerations will be the widest possible extension of personal responsibility; it is the responsible exercise of deliberate choice which most fully expresses personality and best deserves the great name of freedom.

Freedom is the goal of politics. To establish and secure true freedom is the primary object of all right political action. For it is in and through his freedom that a man makes fully real his personality—the quality of one made in the image of God.

Freedom is a great word, and like other great words is often superficially understood. It has been said that to those who have enough of this world's goods the claim to freedom means 'Leave us alone', while to those who have not enough it means 'Give us a chance'. This important difference of interpretation rests on a single understanding of freedom as absence of compulsion or restraint. But if that is all the word means, freedom and futility are likely to be so frequently combined as to seem inseparable. For nothing is so futile as the unhampered satisfaction of sporadic impulses; that is the sort of existence which leads through boredom to suicide. Freedom so far as it is a treasure must be freedom *for* something as well as freedom *from* something. It must be the actual ability to form and carry out a purpose. This implies discipline—at first external discipline to check the wayward impulses before there is a real purpose in life to control them, and afterwards a self-discipline directed to the fulfilment of the purpose of life when formed. Freedom, in short, is self-control, self-determination, self-direction. To train citizens in the capacity for freedom and to give them scope for free action is the supreme end of all true politics.

But man is a self-centred creature. He can be trusted to abuse his freedom. Even so far as he wins self-control, he will control himself in his own interest; not entirely; he is not merely bad; but he is not altogether good, and any fraction of self-centredness will involve the consequence that his purpose conflicts to some extent with that of his neighbour. So there must be the restraint of law, as long as men have any selfishness left in them. Law exists to preserve and extend real freedom. First, it exists to prevent the selfishness of A from destroying the freedom of B. If I am left untouched when I knock my neighbours on the head, their freedom to go about their duties and their pleasures may be greatly diminished. But the law which restrains any occasional homicidal impulse that I may have, by threatening penalties sufficiently disagreeable to make the indulgence of it seem to be not good enough, also protects my purpose of good fellowship against being violated by that same impulse. In such a case the restraint of the law increases the true freedom of all concerned.

(This book is about Social Order and not about conversion or the power of the grace of God. But for the avoidance of confusion I must here remark that no Christian supposes that any one can reach perfect freedom except through perfect faith—that is, a complete personal response to the love of God. Only the love of God working upon his conscience, heart and will can set him free from the self-centredness which otherwise will vitiate both his own life and his contribution to the life of society. This is never completely accomplished, in all probability, for any one at all in this life, certainly not for many; therefore we cannot hope to see the Kingdom of God established in its perfection in this mortal life. That belongs to eternity; but if it is our eternal goal, we have to do all we can to make of history a movement in that direction.

Before passing on it is worth while to notice how absolute was Christ's respect for the freedom of personal choice. He would neither bribe nor coerce men to become followers. Judas must be allowed to betray Him if he is so determined. Not even to save a man from that will the Lord override his freedom. For on freedom all spiritual life utterly depends. It is astonishing and terrifying that the Church has so often failed to understand this. Blindness to it is, as some of us think, the conspicuous defect of Rome to this day, leading to a never repudiated belief in persecution and to a spontaneous sympathy with authoritarian *régimes*. But to use, in the name of Christ, any other means of persuasion than spiritual appeal and rational coherence is to betray His first principle of action.)

## 2. *Social Fellowship*

No man is fitted for an isolated life; every one has needs which he cannot supply for himself; but he needs not only what his neighbours contribute to the equipment of his life but their actual selves as the complement of his own. Man is naturally and incurably social.

Recent political theories have given ostensible emphasis to this truth and have then, as a rule, gone far to ignore it. Certainly our social organization largely ignores it. For this social nature of man is fundamental to his being. I am not first some one on my own account who happens to be the child of my parents, a citizen of Great Britain, and so forth. If you take all these social relationships

away, there is nothing left. A man is talking nonsense if he says:
'Well, if I had been the son of some one else . . . etc.' He *is* his
parents' son; what he is supposing is not that *he* should be some one
else's son, but that *he* should not exist and some one else should
exist instead. By our mutual influence we actually constitute one
another as what we are.[1] This mutual influence finds its first field of
activity in the family; it finds other fields later in school, college,
Trade Union, professional association, city, county, nation,
Church.

Now actual liberty is the freedom which men enjoy in these
various social units. But most political theories confine attention to
the individual and the State as organ of the national community;
they tend to ignore the intermediate groupings. But that makes any
understanding of actual liberty impossible; for it exists for the most
part in and through those intermediate groups—the family, the
Church or congregation, the guild, the Trade Union, the school,
the university, the Mutual Improvement Society. (Only in the
nineteenth century could English people devise such a title as the
last or consent to belong to a society so named; but the thing which
that name quite accurately describes is very common and very
beneficia'.)

It is the common failing of revolutionary politics to ignore or
attempt to destroy these lesser associations. They are nearly always
the product of historical growth and do not quite fit any theoretical
pattern. So the revolutionary, who is of necessity a theorist, is
impatient of them. It was largely for this reason that the great
French Revolution, which took as its watchword Liberty, Equality
and Fraternity, degenerated into a struggle between Liberty and
Equality wherein Fraternity was smothered and Liberty was
judicially murdered. For the isolated citizen cannot effectively be
free over against the State except at the cost of anarchy.

Liberty is actual in the various cultural and commercial and local
associations that men form. In each of these a man can feel that he
counts for something and that others depend on him as he on them.
The State which would serve and guard Liberty will foster all such
groupings, giving them freedom to guide their own activities
provided these fall within the general order of the communal life

and do not injure the freedom of other similar associations. Thus the State becomes the Community of Communities—or rather the administrative organ of that Community—and there is much to be said for the contention that its representative institutions should be so designed as to represent the various groupings of men rather than (or as well as) individuals. To some extent our Parliamentary system does this, with its differentiation of boroughs and shires, and probably Parliament should not go further in this direction. But there is much to be said for the establishment of subordinate functional Councils with powers of action in their several provinces subject to Parliamentary veto—a real Board of Education, for example; an up-to-date Board of Trade which would actually meet!—and above all an Industrial Council with effective powers. To this last we shall return.

In any case the Christian conception of men as members in the family of God forbids the notion that Freedom may be used for self-interest. It is justified only when it expressed itself through fellowship; and a free society must be so organized as to make this effectual; in other words it must be rich in sectional groupings or fellowships within the harmony of the whole.

It is impossible to lay excessive emphasis on this point. Pope Leo XIII gave great prominence to it in the Encyclical *Rerum Novarum*; its prominence there was pointed out with strong approval by Pope Pius XI in *Quadragesimo Anno*; and the profound importance of it has lately been pointed out again by the distinguished French thinker, Jacques Maritain. In his recent book, *Scholasticism and Politics*, he draws a valuable distinction between Personality and Individuality; of course every person is an individual, but his individuality is what marks him off from others; it is a principle of division; whereas personality is social, and only in his social relationships can a man be a person. Indeed, for the completeness of personality, there is needed the relationship to both God and neighbours. The richer his personal relationships, the more fully personal he will be.

This point has great political importance; for these relationships exist in the whole network of communities, associations and fellowships. It is in these that the real wealth of human life consists.

If then it is the function of the State to promote human well-being, it must foster these many groupings of its citizens.

But modern democracy, though more in its continental than in its British forms, was cradled in 'rationalism' with its concepts of the particular and the universal; it was from Rousseau onwards calamitously insensitive to spiritual and cultural affinities. So it has been impatient of these intermediate groupings, and has moved towards 'individualism' or 'collectivism', as if there were no third alternative. But it seems scarcely too much to say that neither individualism nor collectivism is compatible with a truly Christian understanding of man or of life.

In the course of the French Revolution we watch a struggle between a rationalistic and individualist Liberty on the one side and a mechanical and therefore materialist Equality on the other. (The third member of the trio—Fraternity—was not engaged in this conflict, and found its chief expression in the unity so useful for fighting those who were not of the brotherhood.) In the end both Liberty and Equality were suppressed by the triumphant Absolutism of Napoleon.

The English history of Freedom is different from this continental movement towards Liberty such as we have described. Freedom here—as in Holland—has its origin chiefly in the claim of Dissenters from the Established Church to worship God as their consciences might direct. It was rooted in faith. Hence the great Dutch social philosophy has more than any other laid stress upon the State as the Community of communities.[2]

A democracy which is to be Christian must be a democracy of persons, not only of individuals. It must not only tolerate but encourage minor communities as at once the expression and the arena of personal freedom; and its structure must be such as to serve this end. That is the partial justification of Fascism which has made its triumphs possible. It sins far more deeply against true freedom than it supports it; yet in the materialist and mechanical quality of the democratic movement from Rousseau to Karl Marx and his communist disciples, it had real justification for reacting against them.

It is impossible to say how much we owe in our own country to the schooling in democratic habits provided, first by the old Trade Guilds, then, when the fellowship of trade had been broken up by the release of individualist acquisitiveness, by the Trade Unions, and ever since the seventeenth century by the dissenting congregations. Many of our most effective Labour leaders learned their art of public speech as local preachers; and the self-government of the local Chapel has been a fruitful school of democratic procedure. Our 'Left Wing' has by no means always maintained this close association of democratic principle with conscientious worship of God! But the historical root is there. And the British tradition of freedom has probably more of the element which consists of the claim to obey God rather than men and less of the element of mere self-assertiveness than has the democratic tradition in most other countries. The element of self-assertiveness is morally bad and politically disastrous; a freedom based upon it is only an opportunity for selfishness and will decline through anarchy to disruption of the State; the claim to obey God rather than men is a source both of moral strength, for it inspires devotion to duty, and of political stability, for such freedom may only be used in the service of the whole fellowship.

### 3. *Service*

The combination of Freedom and Fellowship as principles of social life issues in the obligation of Service. No one doubts this in so far as it concerns the individual. Whatever our practice may be, we all give lip-service to this principle.

Its application to the individual is pretty clear. It affects him in two main ways—as regards work and leisure. In England we have depended a great deal on voluntary service given in leisure hours. We want a great deal more of it; and we have a right to expect more than we get from the Christian Churches. Yet it is certain that a very large proportion of the day-to-day drudgery of social service is done by Christian men and women in the inspiration of their Christian faith. We want more of them; but the greater part of what is done at all is done by Christian folk.

What is less often recognized in practice is the obligation to make of the occupation, by which a man or woman earns a living, a sphere of service. This may be done in two ways. Some young people have the opportunity to choose the kind of work by which they will earn their living. To make that choice on selfish grounds is probably the greatest single sin that any young person can commit, for it is the deliberate withdrawal from allegiance to God of the greatest part of time and strength. This does not mean that no attention is to be paid to inclinations. Inclination is often a true guide to vocation; for we like doing what we can do well, and we shall give our best service by giving scope to our own aptitudes and talents. But a young man who is led by his inclination to take up teaching or business or whatever it may be, must none the less make his choice because in that field he can give his own best service. This will enormously affect the spirit in which he does his work and his dealings with the other people engaged in it or with whom it brings him into contact. Let no one say that this has no application to modern business; there are many men engaged in business to-day, and leaders of industry on the largest scale, who entered on their work in this spirit of service and have maintained that spirit in the conduct of their business.

But there are many for whom there seems to be little choice; life offers one opening and no more; or they have to take what the Labour Exchange can suggest. For them it is harder to find in daily work a true vocation; but it is not impossible. Circumstances as well as inclination may be the channel through which God's call comes to a man. And His call is sometimes to self-sacrifice as well as to self-fulfilment. (No doubt self-sacrifice is in the end the truest self-fulfilment, as Christianity alone of religions or ethical systems teaches. And this explains how it may happen that the God of love calls men to self-sacrifice.) It is possible to accept the one job available, however distasteful and dreary, as God's call to me; and then I shall enter on it in the spirit of service.

Of course, this does not justify an order of society which offers to many men only such forms of livelihood as require a miracle of grace to appear as forms of true vocation. But we must recognize that the source of my vocation is in God and not in me. It is His call to me. And when it is said that we need to create or restore a sense of vocation in relation to all the activities of men, it does not mean chiefly that every individual should be able to find there his self-expression or self-fulfilment otherwise than by self-sacrifice. But it does mean, first that he should do his work, interesting or dreary, 'as unto the Lord', and secondly that the alternatives presented be such as shall not make this insuperably difficult apart from a true miracle of grace.

It is not only individuals who must, if Christianity is the truth, guide their policy or career by the principle of service; all groupings of men must do the same. The rule here should be that we use our wider loyalties to check the narrower. A man is a member of his family, of his nation, and of mankind. It is very seldom that anyone can render a service directly to mankind as a whole. We serve mankind by serving those parts of it with which we are closely connected. And our narrower loyalties are likely to be more intense than the wider, and therefore call out more devotion and more strenuous effort. But we can and should check these keener, narrower loyalties by recognizing the prior claim of the wider. So a man rightly does his best for the welfare of his own family, but must never serve his family in ways that injure the nation. A man rightly does his best for his country, but must never serve his country in ways that injure mankind.

Of course, this apparent collision of claims will not arise so far as he accepts in its completeness the Christian standard of values; for in that scale of values service itself, even at cost of real sacrifice, is highest. But no man can in fact apply this exacting code, and it is of the utmost importance that we recognize this inability and the reasons for it.

A man cannot regulate his service of his family and of his country by the Christian scale of values in its purity, first because he does not effectively accept it for himself, and secondly because his family and country do not accept it. Nothing is so offensive as a man who applies a higher standard to other people than to himself. If a man says to his children: 'I might have given you an expensive education, but decided that it would be better for you to go to the freely provided State school because my Christian principles teach me that wealth ought not to confer privilege', he must show in his whole life that he sets no store by the advantages which money can buy; otherwise he will only be stingy and his account of his conduct will be hypocrisy, or (as we call it nowadays) 'rationalization'. Now no one does accept the Christian standard for himself; that Jesus of Nazareth did so is precisely what constitutes the gulf between Him and all other men. Only a perfect Christian can follow the purely Christian way of life; and so far as an imperfect Christian—i.e. any Christian who actually exists—forces himself to a line of conduct which his own character does not support, it will have bad effects on both him and his neighbours: on him, because it will be an assertion of self-will and must root him more firmly than ever in his own self as centre of his life, that is in his Original Sin: and on others. because he will appear as a Pharisee and a prig, and will alienate people from the standard by which he is self-righteously guiding this part of his conduct.

(I am finding it very hard to write this book about Christianity and the Social Order without bringing in everything else. Here I will content myself with one recollection. When a man asked St. Augustine, 'What must I do to be saved?' he answered, 'Love God and do what you like'—because, of course, if he loved God he would like and could do the right thing, and if he did not love God he could not do it however much he tried.)

But it is not only his own defect of Christianity that a man must consider. He must not force its standard on others who are as yet unwilling or unable to receive it; for it is of the essence of spiritual faith that it be freely accepted. If a man applies in the training of his children standards not generally accepted in their circle, and fails to bring the children themselves to accept them, the result is likely to be an alienation of the children, both from their father and from his standards.

That is one obvious illustration of the difficulty presented by the claim that Christian standards should regulate our conduct. Of course they should, but they must first regulate our souls; and even then they are to be followed in that way—and in that way only—which will, in fact, secure a result truly expressive of them.

We see then why a man cannot without more ado take as his guide for the treatment of his fellows the Christian standard that service to the point of self-sacrifice is our truest welfare. Let him live by that as far as he can; and let him invite others to join him in that enterprise; but let him not force that standard on his fellows, and least of all on those dependent on him. They will always have the opportunity to act on it if they are so minded.

The general rule in such matters must be very general indeed, and gives little help beyond an indication of the direction in which we must move. A man must chiefly serve his own most immediate community, accepting as the standard of its welfare that which its members are ready to accept (though trying, it may be, to lead them nearer to a fully Christian view), but always checking this narrower service by the wider claims, so that in serving the smaller community he never injures the larger.

But as a member of each small group—with a voice in determining its conduct and policy—e.g. as a Christian Trade Unionist or Managing Director, or as the Governor of a School—he will do all he can to secure that his own group accepts for itself the principle of service and sets its course in the way that will benefit not only its own members in their own self-interest, but also the larger community in which this group is a part.

Freedom, Fellowship, Service—these are the three principles of a Christian social order, derived from the still more fundamental Christian postulates that Man is a child of God and is destined for a life of eternal fellowship with Him.

# 6

## *The Natural Order and the Priority of Principles*

One of our great needs is some general system of thought or map of the intellectual world by which we may be helped to judge which of several principles should prevail when it is impossible to give full expression to all. Incidentally, it may be worth while to observe that our duty in this field is seldom to adopt one principle and see it through. Controversialists often demand this in the name of logic or of consistency. But the first requirement of a sane logic is that we should consider what principles are involved and how we may do the fullest justice to them all. Thus, if we say that we stand for equality of opportunity, some one is almost sure to say, 'Very well; but do be consistent and abolish the family'. Of course it is true that so long as children are brought up in their own families, they will not have equal opportunities, for some families will stimulate and others will suffocate their intellectual or other interests. But equality of opportunity is only one among several principles that should find expression in the training of young citizens; and the real problem is to ascertain, as far as may be, all the principles and then combine them as fully as possible.

It is possible that my discussion of Christian social principles in the last two chapters may be criticized for omitting the two most important of all—Justice and Love. But these are principles of another order. They have their place in this field chiefly as regulating those which I have already described. It is axiomatic that Love should be the predominant Christian impulse, and that the primary form of Love in social organization is Justice. No doubt this latter truth is sometimes ignored by those who wish to apply Love, so to speak, wholesale and direct. But it is hard to see how this works out. Imagine a Trade Union Committee negotiating with an Employers' Federation in an industrial crisis on the verge of a strike or lock-out. This Committee is to be actuated by love. Oh, yes, by all means—but towards whom? Are they to love the workers or the employers? Of course—both. But then that will not help them much to determine what terms ought to be either proposed or accepted. The fact is that these problems arise only so far as perfect love is not operative. That is a reason why both sides should confess their sin, but still the problem is unsolved. Love, in fact, finds its primary expression through Justice—which in the field of industrial disputes means in practice that each side should state its own case as strongly as it can before the most impartial tribunal available, with determination to accept the award of that tribunal. At least that puts the two parties on a level, and is to that extent in accord with the command, 'Thou shalt love thy neighbour as thyself'.

But as Love can find expression only through Justice, so Justice is incapable of any definition which renders it applicable to actual circumstances by any rule of thumb. Perhaps the old formula that Justice consists in rendering to every one his due is as good as any, though readers of Plato's *Republic* will recall the curious results which skilful dialectic can extract from it. But what is due to a man? How do we judge? In time of war the cost of living rises; there is a demand for a rise in wages to meet this. How do we decide whether that demand is just, and if it is how great the rise should be? We try to apply the principle of equality of sacrifice; but how do we measure sacrifice? One man may lose without feeling it a sum of which the loss would be crippling to another. And numerical proportion, though better than numerical equality, is still unsatisfactory. There seems no way except to put the problem before a fair-minded man who is able to see all round the question, and then trust his judgement, which will be one of feeling—of course, the feeling of a disciplined mind—rather than of calculation.

These two great principles then—Love and Justice—must be

rather regulative of our application of other principles than taken as immediate guides to social policy. But they must constantly be borne in mind as checks upon policy. As we must use our wider loyalties to check the narrower, so we must use these highest principles of all to check our application of the lower. Freedom must not be pursued in ways which offend against Love, nor must service be demanded, or fellowship in any actual instance promoted, in ways that offend against Justice.

In earlier times, Christian thinkers made great use of the notion of Natural Law. They did not mean by this a generalization from a large number of observed phenomena, which is what a modern scientist means; they meant the proper function of a human activity as apprehended by a consideration of its own nature. In practice, the Natural Order or Natural Law is discovered partly by observing the generally accepted standards of judgement and partly by consideration of the proper functions of whatever is the subject of enquiry. This is a task for human reason; but so far as reason enables us to reach the truth about anything in its own essence and in its relationships, it enables us to see it as it is in the mind of God. Thus it is a Natural, not a Supernatural, Order with which we are concerned; but as God is the Creator, this Natural Order is His order and its law is His law.

Thus, in the economic field, the reason why goods are produced is that men may satisfy their needs by consuming those goods. Production by its own natural law exists for consumption. If, then, a system comes into being in which production is regulated more by the profit obtainable for the producer than by the needs of the consumer, that system is defying the Natural Law or Natural Order.

There is nothing wrong about profits as such. It has always been recognized that both the producer and the trader are entitled to a profit as their own means of livelihood, which they have earned by their service to the community. Further, there can be no profit except so far as the needs of consumers are being met. But it is possible none the less for these two to get into the wrong order, so that the consumer is treated, not as the person whose interest is the true end of the whole process, but only as an indispensable condition of success in an essentially profit-seeking enterprise.

Now if the economic process is isolated, this may not make much difference. It is quite conceivable that a system which falls under censure for its breach of the 'Natural Order' should none the less be extremely effective in providing a high standard of life for a very large number of people. Whether or not our existing form of Capitalism in Great Britain offends against 'Natural Law', it has certainly given to the mass of the people a higher standard of life—a larger enjoyment of material goods—than any previous system. Moreover, it seems nearly certain that no other system would have developed so rapidly or so far the new powers conferred by modern science. If we treat the economic activity of man as an independent sphere, to be judged only by its own canons of effectiveness in the production and distribution of goods, criticism based on any conception of a Natural Order or Natural Law will seem very academic and remote.

No doubt there are signs that the system may be about to fail at the point of distribution; we shall return to that in the next chapter when we use our general understanding of Social Order as a critique by which to estimate our own social order. And if it be true that the system is moving by the development of its own inherent logic towards its own breakdown, that will be strong evidence both that there is a Natural Order and that our system in part violates it.

But the believer in Natural Order has another shot in his locker. For he refuses to admit that the economic activity of man may be thus isolated and judged by its own canons alone. Certainly there is a real technical autonomy in this as in every other department, and neither theology nor ethics can determine the probable economic effects of any proposed economic reform—as for example whether in a given instance the imposition of a tariff will raise prices. In the region of causes and effects, economic science is autonomous. But according to Natural Law the economic process is not an end in itself; it and all its parts are primarily a means to something that is much more than economic—the life of man.

Now man is a child of God, destined for eternal fellowship with Him, though a sinful child who in many ways frustrates his own destiny. Further, as children of God, men and women are members of one family, and their true development is that of an ever richer personal experience in an ever wider and deeper fellowship. If, then, an economic system is abundantly effective in producing and distributing material goods, but creates or intensifies divisions and hostilities between men, that system is condemned, not on economic but on moral grounds; not because it fails to deliver the goods, but because it is a source of wrong personal relationships.

The old conception of Natural Law has lost much of its appeal for us through the fact that it was worked out in special relation to a feudal and peasant society. The forms of that society are vanished; but it embodies some important principles, of which perhaps the chief is the close association of status, and of wealth as conferring status, with social function. Each man had his place in the scheme—whether this was the bare security (with very little freedom) of the serf, or the power enjoyed by the baron in virtue of service rendered or liable to be claimed. There was no recognition of irresponsible power, such as may now be wielded by the inheritors of great wealth, either in land or in industrial shares.[1] But the basic principles were concealed behind their temporary applications, so when urban civilization began to rival the old peasant type and then to supersede it, and when under its pressure Calvin granted a qualified indulgence to usury, the old principles were rapidly forgotten, and we are now faced with the difficulty of re-asserting them in a world developed in almost complete independence of them.

It is wholesome to go back to this conception of Natural Law because it holds together two aspects of truth which it is not easy to hold in combination—the ideal and the practical. We tend to follow one or other of two lines: either we start from a purely ideal conception, and then we bleat fatuously about love; or else we start from the world as it is with the hope of remedying an abuse here or there, and then we have no general direction or criterion of progress. The conception of Natural Law will help us to frame a conception of the right or ideal relation between the various activities of men and of the men engaged in them. For consideration of the status of an activity in the light of its social function keeps both the ideal and the practical full in view.

Thus we shall recognize at once and fully both the truth that production exists for consumption, and the other truth that unless he makes a profit the producer cannot survive. (There may be commodities which it is desirable on social grounds to provide at cost price or even less; if so, the State should subsidize them, whether it takes over the ownership of them or not. It might be profitable to the community as a whole to supply transport of certain kinds of goods at a very low rate—e.g. perishable fruits in their season. But someone must pay; if it is the whole community that gains, the whole community should pay.) Now it is always true that a *conditio sine qua non* is more indispensable to an undertaking than its goal. If there is no profit for the producer, production will cease, whereas it can still go on even though the interest of the consumer is comparatively little regarded. Even if all production were taken over by the State, it would still be true that it would have as a whole to earn a profit, though loss on one department could be set off by gains in others. So we get this general position: for economic production there *must* be profits, there *ought* to be regard for the consumer's interest, and it is wrong to sacrifice that interest to the increase of profits above a reasonable figure.

So it is with regard to the relation of the economic to the cultural life of man. The economic is the more indispensable; if men starve they can neither write poetry nor enjoy it. Yet the economic exists to subserve the cultural. The whole equipment of life with food, houses, clothes, furniture and so forth is for the sake of the personal life, the family life, the cultural development, the human fellowship which is thus made possible. That which is only a means is indispensable; the true end of life can be forgone, yet the means remains means and the end remains end; and the means (industry, commerce, etc.) is to be judged by its success in promoting or facilitating the true ends of human life—religion, art, science and, above all, happy human relationships.

In the same way we must relate together freedom and order. Order is to be valued as the basis of freedom; only in a well ordered society are the members of society really free. If the roads are beset by highwaymen we are not free to travel. Freedom is a finer thing than order, but order is more indispensable than freedom. If freedom is so developed as to turn into anarchy and chaos, men will always accept the alternative of tyranny in hope that order may be restored.

The conservative temperament tends to dwell on what is indispensable, that this may be safeguarded. The radical temperament tends to dwell most on the higher ends of life, that these may be facilitated. The world needs both. But wisdom consists in the union of the two. The great advantage of the conception of Natural Law is that it leads us to consider every activity in its context in the whole economy of life, and so to grasp the vital importance of safeguarding what is indispensable while we fulfil the obligation of reaching out towards the higher ends as yet imperfectly attained.

# 7

## *The Task Before Us*

So far we have been occupied with general considerations, trying to ascertain what are the principles that should guide us in handling the social and economic problems of our time. Those problems were urgent enough before the war; the war has vastly increased their urgency. When it is over, the interest on the National Debt will be a heavy burden and a serious drain on our resources, and there will be the need to reconstruct the devastated areas of many towns with all the adjustment of rights, vested interests and social welfare which any planning must involve. The structure of life as we knew it before the war has already been profoundly modified. How far do we want to restore it if we can? In which respects is it desirable that it should be changed in its inner principle?

One of the most widely read books of recent years has been Peter Drucker's *The End of Economic Man*. It may be argued that he exaggerates the extent to which human life had come, by the beginning of the twentieth century, to be dominated by economic considerations. But it is not open to dispute that these occupied a greater place in the ordering of life and the shaping of individual ambitions than in any previous period. The immense possibilities opened up by the application of 'power'—water, steam, electricity—to industrial production so fascinated men that they ceased to ask what was the purpose of this vast mass of production. It tended to be an end in itself. It was no longer subordinated to the general scheme of a complete human life in which it should be a part.

Let us test this by some of the principles by which the Christian tradition would lead us to direct human life.

(1) *The Family as the Primary Social Unit*—If this principle is admitted some results immediately follow. A community committed to this principle would see that there were houses available for all citizens, within their means, in which a family could be brought up in health and happiness, in the unity of family life and in the decency and dignity proper to human beings who are the children of God. But the supply of houses, as of other commodities, was until very lately left to private enterprise, and the *entrepreneur* carried out his functions not with a primary regard to the needs of the people but with a view to the profit which he could make. He is not to be blamed for this; there is nothing wrong about profits as such, and the private builder or firm cannot carry on at all unless there results a profit to supply a livelihood. But the result has been horrible overcrowding and all the horror of slums. It is not the builders who are to blame; it is the public. We ought to have felt a responsibility in the matter, and most of us felt none. Now at any rate we must secure a public opinion which will lay it upon Government as a primary obligation to see that the housing necessary to healthy family life is available for all citizens. Great strides were taken before the war broke out; but the goal is not yet reached.

Family life involves some leisure which the members of the family may spend together. In these days hours of work are seldom excessive, unless the occupation is so monotonous that for this reason the period spent in it should be reduced. But it seldom appears as though the unity of the family were one of the considerations kept in mind in the planning of a 'shift' system; it cannot be claimed that in this matter it should be decisive, but it ought not to be forgotten as it would seem very often to be in industry to-day.

There must be some periods of greater and fuller opportunity for united family enjoyment than leisure on working-days can give, or even that Sunday which can be so precious in the life of any family. Holidays have a great part of their meaning and value in the fact that they give this fuller opportunity; but it will be less than it should be if there is anxiety about the money. Either wages should be high enough to enable a man to put by what he will need for full and free enjoyment with his wife and children during the holiday, or payment must be continued throughout. The latter is the right principle, for a holiday ought not to be regarded as a time away from industry but as a time of recuperation for better service, so that industry itself is interested to promote it; holidays with pay should be a universally accepted principle.

Real extravagance is always wrong. But to splash about a little on holiday is thoroughly right. It is not only permissible; it is a duty.

But even though payment is continued through holidays, it must be sufficient at other times to ensure the possibility of a good upbringing for the children. Here there is a real difficulty. The care of his children is a man's natural responsibility. Yet it is difficult to say that every man, even though unmarried, should be paid at a rate needed by another man who has six children. The economic case for Family Allowances seems unanswerable. Of course they must be paid by the State, not by the industry—for if the industry has to meet this charge it will tend to employ unmarried or childless men.

At present there is urgent need to attend to this matter, for many children are under-nourished. But that theme connects with our next principle as well as with the family.

(2) *The Sanctity of Personality*—Our established order of life recognizes the sanctity of Personality in many ways. We have freedom of thought and speech in England, at least in the sense of absence of legal restrictions upon them, such as has seldom been achieved in any nation. We have freedom within the law and equality before the law—except so far as the cost of litigation may interfere with this equality. But in one great department of life the principle receives scanty recognition. When the new industry began, about a century and a half ago, the pioneers showed little respect for the personality of those who earned their living by working in factories and mills. They were often called 'hands'; and a hand is by nature a 'living tool', which is the classical definition of a slave. The worst horrors of the early factories have been abolished, but the wage earners are not yet fully recognized as persons. For the supreme mark of a person is that he orders his life

by his own deliberate choice; and the 'workers' usually have no voice in the control of the industry whose requirements determine so large a part of their lives. How such a voice is to be found for them, and when, are questions for the expert to answer; but industry will not be free from the charge of neglecting this principle until in some form labour shares at least equally with capital in the control of industry.

But our regard for this principle must carry us further back than this. The foundation of personal life is the body and its powers. Respect for the sacredness of Personality in all citizens will lead us to demand that no child shall be condemned to grow to maturity with faculties stunted by malnutrition or by lack of opportunities for full development. We have made great progress in these matters, but there is need for very much more. Sir John Orr declared a few years ago that 'the diet of nearly one half of the population is deficient for health'. And if children suffer from malnutrition, so do adolescents from lack of appropriate outdoor exercise for the development of their physique. The loss from these two causes is not only physical; an under-nourished and under-developed body is likely to house an irritable, querulous and defensive soul. We have begun to attend to these two matters; but we had long neglected them, and now our attention to them is no more than languid.

At this point also our whole educational system comes under condemnation as defective and inadequate.

In the present connexion the chief evils of our educational system seem to be two: the size of classes in many elementary schools, and the age at which school education for most boys and girls comes to an end.

The excessive size of classes makes impossible any proper attention to individuals. The teacher has to spend a great amount of ingenuity and skill in retaining the attention of the whole crowd, and it is only rarely that the children can be set to work by themselves while the teacher takes them one by one correcting mistakes and offering suggestions. Plainly such a method fails to do justice to the individuality of the various children. In other words, it fails to apply in this sphere our principle of the sacredness of individual personality. One of the reforms for which we must make the most urgent demand, as soon as the war is over, is the still further reduction of the size of classes in elementary schools.

The main ground for the raising of the school age is often obscured by other considerations which are important in their place, but are essentially secondary. This main ground is the necessity of providing a social life or community in which the individual may feel that he has a real share and for which he may feel some genuine responsibility. If a child is thrown out into the world at fourteen or even fifteen with nothing to which he may belong between him and the national community, or even his city or county, that is too large a body for him to realize in it anything like living membership. He needs a society of people about his own age, in the activities of which he may take a share equal to that of any other member, so that it may reasonably claim his loyalty, and he may have the sense of being wanted in it. Nothing else will draw out from him the latent possibilities of his nature. At present this need is supplied by voluntary organizations, sometimes in an admirable manner, to a small proportion of the young population. But it appears that 80 per cent of young people between fourteen and twenty have no connexion with any such organization, and in any case the organizations can only operate in the leisure time of the boys and girls. Of course it is true that if the school-age is to be raised, we need a far more varied type of education, and for a great many, probably the large majority, this ought to consist much more in various forms of manual activity than in the extraction of information from printed books; there might be a system of apprenticeship to various industries, especially agriculture, under the supervision of the Local Education Authority and its officers. But there is no chance of our developing this varied curriculum, or training teachers to handle it, until the thing begins to be done. We must start with inadequate equipment and then make it more adequate as we go on. When once it is granted that the main need of the young citizen is a living fellowship of other young citizens within which the greater part of his time shall be spent, criticisms of the available forms of curriculum become irrelevant to the main issue. If we are going to show a real respect for each individual as a child of God, we must see that from infancy to full maturity every child is set in such a social context as will best develop all the powers which God has given him. To provide such an opportunity, not for a favoured few but for all children, is an urgent national duty. To fail here on the ground of the large expenditure required would be a national sin.

(3) *The Principle of Fellowship*—Our discussion of the former principle has already led us up to fellowship, which is at once an inherent need of human nature and the means through which the best things possible to men are realized. We have so far spoken of the school, and especially the secondary school, as the fellowship in which the individual can be brought to fullest maturity. We now turn to the other aspect of the same truth in order to insist that this maturity itself includes growth in fellowship. The development of individual gifts under a predominant motive of self-seeking is an injury both to the individual and to the society. Plato saw this perfectly clearly. It was only those who had been moulded by his moral training who would in his ideal Republic be allowed to receive higher intellectual equipment. In other words, if a man is going to be a knave, it is desirable both for society and for himself that he should also be a fool. To quicken the wits of those who will afterwards use them to prey upon their neighbours is an evident injury to society, but it is a still greater injury to them. In the past our State System paid little attention to this aspect of the matter. When education was first made universal this was done by the erection of great buildings, of which Charles Masterman truly said that they 'proclaim by the very audacity of their ferocious ugliness the advantages of State-given eduction'. They were, in fact, mere boxes of class-rooms. The whole suggestion was that children must be educated all together because it was too expensive to educate them separately. Again, each child was free to leave on its birthday at the school-leaving age, irrespective of the stage reached in the life of the school; it might be after the first week of a term. No account was taken of the life of the school as itself a living community. The teachers have been steadily correcting this for a long time past and have done wonders, considering the difficulties confronting them. Now for a good many years the Authorities have

also begun to see the real perspectives in this matter, and some are taking pains to make school buildings not only commodious but beautiful, and are, in many ways, encouraging the school's corporate life. There is still room for a great deal of development in this direction, but our feet are set on the right way.

But there is one great division in our educational scheme. The so-called Public Schools, which have held the corporate tradition strongly throughout their long history, have been inaccessible to the poorer children. This was probably inevitable in a period when education as a whole had become a perquisite of the wealthier section of society. It is on the way to being a shocking anomaly as education is made available to the whole community. That what is generally felt to be the best form of education should be reserved to those whose parents are able to pay expensive fees, or expensive preparatory school education with a view to the winning of scholarships, makes a cleavage in the educational and social life of the country as a whole, which is itself destructive of the best fellowship. The time is ripe for a development by which it should be possible for children from every kind of home to come into any kind of school provided that they are qualified by mental, physical and personal talents. The test must not be purely intellectual. We have overstressed the intellectual element in recent educational developments, and the competitive examination system has tended to favour many who have been most industrious and have capable brains, but sacrifice to the development of these all other gifts and aptitudes. We need fully balanced people of well developed bodies and wide personal contacts and interests, as well as quickened imagination and diciplined intelligence; but it is possible to devise tests of these qualities, and admission to the best types of school should in future depend upon the combination of such tests.

If, however, this great stress is to be laid upon the corporate life of the school, it becomes of great importance to secure that the corporate life itself is healthy. It seems that there are here only two alternatives—for the mere existence of the corporate life excludes the possibility of pure individualism. This strong corporate life will act as a mould forcing all who share in it to conform to one pattern, unless it is known and felt to be a preparation for something larger than itself. The 'Public Schools' are often criticized for suppressing individuality; the criticism, when expressed at all, is usually exaggerated, but it has some foundation in fact. These schools do impart a genuinely public spirit, but do this with something of that class-reference which is inherent in their present character as based on financial privilege. If they are felt to be rooted in the whole nation rather than in one section of it, this criticism will lose its relevance.

But it is quite possible to develop in a school a very strong corporate life by methods which crush out individuality, whether the corporate life of the school is treated as an end in itself or is dedicated to something beyond itself. It follows that the further object which the school is known to serve must be of such a kind as to foster individual development on the one hand and world-fellowship on the other; it must offer an allegiance which calls forth instead of suppressing individuality and creates bonds of union with all fellow-citizens and with citizens of all other nations. There is only one candidate for this double function: it is Christianity. We must then take steps to secure that the corporate life of the schools is Christian.

This means much more than the inclusion of Christian doctrine in the curriculum, though without this the goal could not be reached. There must be regular corporate worship, and the atmosphere of the school must be as far as possible Christian. Service of the community must be the chief title to honour; and the school community itself should undertake such forms of service as are practicable to the wider community in which it is situated or to the less fortunate members thereof. The periods of Christian instruction and worship should be felt—unconsciously if not consciously—as bringing to a focus what is the spirit of the whole school-community; and to that end the life of the school should be so planned that Christian teaching and worship is indeed its focus.

We are dealing with Christianity and Social Order and cannot discuss Education in all its aspects. But we are not training children according to their own true nature or in relation to their true environment unless we are training them to trust in God. In their own nature they are God's children, destined for eternal fellowship with Him; and their environment exists at three levels—the sub-human, studied in the Natural Sciences; the human, studied in the Humanities; and the super-human, studied in Divinity. The school must provide for all three.

What a school can accomplish is very little, unless it is working in alliance with the stronger influences of the home and of society at large. How far does the ordering of social life as we know it express and inculcate this principle of Fellowship?

To a great extent it does. As compared with some other countries or with our own at other times, we find in the British people a magnificent unity. In many parts of the countryside, especially where the old families have kept their estates and live among the people, there is often a genuine social fellowship and a real personal equality on the basis of an accepted differentiation of function. For example, I treasure the memory of the elderly farmer on the Garrowby estate who, meeting Lord Halifax for the first time after he had become Foreign Secretary, patted him on the arm and said: 'Ye've made a good start; keep it oop.' And in the industrial world, especially in family firms, there is sometimes a real and admirable fellowship of employer and employed. I remember, for example, the Works Committee of an engineering firm in Manchester at which an operative said: 'Well, if there's no particular business to-day, Mr. Chairman, I've got a question to ask: 'What about this 'ere Predestination?' To which the Chairman replied: 'I should like notice of that question, and I'll ask the Bishop'—which explains how I came into it.

Yet allowing for all this, the breaches in our fellowship are pretty serious. Our snobbery as a nation is, I suppose, without parallel; it is worst in suburbia; but it is bad in most parts of society and at every level; and our educational methods tend to intensify it. In the world of industry as a whole, despite admirable exceptions, the division between Labour, Management and Capital is very wide and deep. At this point, however, we should take note of a new factor in the situation which is full of hope. 'Management' is fast becoming a profession, with its own standards and its own objectives. Its primary interest is not dividends for the shareholders, but efficiency of service. Profits are for it not so much a source of income—for Managers receive a fixed salary which is part of the cost of production—but an index of efficiency. The sympathy of Managers is usually with Labour, though the terms of their appointment tend to class them with Capital. Some adjustment at this point might have very great results.

The existing system has many triumphs to its credit; it has raised the standard of life for the common people to a level never reached before. The life of the 'working people' is for the most part neither impoverished, nor over-burdensome, nor lacking in interest. But it suffers from one great lack, from one common evil, and from one terrible menace. The great lack is the absence of any voice in the control or direction of the concern to which most of the waking hours of the day are given. Till this can be remedied there will be one most important respect in which the working class is shut out from a vitally important expression of personality. Men have fought and died for a voice in making the laws which they are to obey; that is the essence of political liberty. But the government of the firm for which he works affects a man's life more closely than the Government of his State; yet in it he has no part except so far as he may threaten to hold up the process by withdrawing his labour and that of his fellow-workers in a strike. In many businesses nowadays the workers are often consulted, especially about regulations affecting hours and conditions of work. So far, so good; but this is done as of favour and not as a matter of secured right. The cause of freedom will not be established till political freedom is fulfilled in economic freedom.

Moreover, until this is done, the breach in the fellowship—of which the class-war is the ultimate expression—must remain. It is important to remember that the class-war was not first proclaimed as a crusade by Marx and Engels; it was first announced as a fact by Adam Smith. Nothing can securely end it except the acquisition by Labour of a share in the control of industry. Capital gets its dividends; Labour gets its wages; there is no reason why Capital should also get control and Labour have no share in it, except that hitherto Capital had education and Labour had not; but that defect in the equipment of Labour is well on the way to being remedied.

A great evil afflicting many in modern industry is that the work required of them is so monotonous and engages so few human faculties that it is hard for a man to find in it any real vocation. It is true that there is often some misunderstanding here. People sometimes speak as if finding a vocation in one's work were the same thing as finding in it self-expression or self-fulfilment; but God's calling or vocation for us may very well be to self-sacrifice; and for a perfect saint it might be possible to perform the most wearisome and monotonous task 'as unto God' because it was his contribution to human welfare. But to ask any ordinary man so to regard monotonous drudgery occupying the whole of a working day is sheer mockery. He cannot so regard it; and if so, the conditions of his work are making it impossible for him to worship in any full sense. For worship is the offer of our whole being and life—therefore very prominently our work—to God; and no one but an already perfect saint could sincerely offer that sort of work to God.

When Moses observed the conditions in which Israelites were working in Egypt he did not say: 'Your surroundings are drab and your work dreary; you shall have a specially beautiful Church to lift your thoughts above these mundane cares to heaven'; he said: 'We can't worship God here; we must get away from it.'

The worst evil afflicting the working-class in England is insecurity; they live under the terrible menace of unemployment. And in our own time a new and horrible evil has appeared—long-term unemployment on a considerable scale. Unemployment is a corrosive poison. It saps both physical and moral strength. The worst effect of it, especially now that the community takes some care of its unemployed members, is not the physical want, but the moral disaster of not being wanted. This brings most misery to the mature man who has been in regular work for many years and relies on it as the framework of his life; but it does most harm to the young man who never forms habits of regular work at all.

Now it is no part of the duty of a Christian as such to draw plans of a reformed society. But it is part of his duty to know and proclaim Christian principles, to denounce as evil what contravenes them, and to insist that these evils should be remedied. Further, it is his duty to judge how far particular evils are symptoms of a disease deeper than themselves, and if that seems to be so to ask how far the whole existing order is contrary to the Natural Order.

It seems clear that such evils as we have mentioned cannot be due to mere lack of goodwill. For there is an abundance of goodwill. Some deeper cause must be sought. So we are led to ask how far it is true that our existing order corresponds to the Natural Order. How far, for example, is it true that the primary concern of those who control production is so to direct it that all engaged in it find in their activity a truly human life, and that the needs of the public are met? How often are these questions discussed at Boards of Directors? Is it not evident that the primary concern is for profits out of which dividends may be paid to shareholders? Of course there must be profits; without them the industry must close down, workers fall into unemployment and shareholders lose their capital. Also, of course, it is only through supplying the needs of consumers that the producers can make those necessary profits. But the consumer ought not to come in only or chiefly as a means to the interest of the producer; his interest ought to be paramount. For in the Natural Order consumption is the end of production.

As I write it is frequently reported that so soon as the price of a commodity is fixed by the Ministry of Food, it disappears from the market. Why?

To many it appears evident that we have allowed the making of profits, which is necessary as a means to the continuance of the industry, to get into the first place which properly belongs to the supply of human needs—the true end of industry. We have inverted the 'natural order.' Instead of finance existing to facilitate production and production existing to supply needs, the supply of needs is made the means to profitable production; and production itself is controlled as much as it is facilitated by finance.

If that is true, it is the duty of Christians to become aware of it and to demand a remedy. It cannot be said that it is their duty as Christians to know what the remedy is, for this involves many technical matters. But they are entitled to call upon the Government to set before itself the following objectives and pursue them as steadily and rapidly as opportunity permits:

1. Every child should find itself a member of a family housed with

decency and dignity, so that it may grow up as a member of that basic community in a happy fellowship unspoilt by underfeeding or overcrowding, by dirty and drab surroundings or by mechanical monotony of environment.

2. Every child should have the opportunity of an education till years of maturity, so planned as to allow for his peculiar aptitudes and make possible their full development. This education should throughout be inspired by faith in God and find its focus in worship.

3. Every citizen should be secure in possession of such income as will enable him to maintain a home and bring up children in such conditions as are described in paragraph 1 above.

4. Every citizen should have a voice in the conduct of the business or industry which is carried on by means of his labour, and the satisfaction of knowing that his labour is directed to the well-being of the community.

5. Every citizen should have sufficient daily leisure, with two days of rest in seven, and, if an employee, an annual holiday with pay, to enable him to enjoy a full personal life with such interests and activities as his tasks and talents may direct.

6. Every citizen should have assured liberty in the forms of freedom of worship, of speech, of assembly, and of association for special purposes.

As a background to these six points we need to insist on the principle laid down by the four religious leaders in their Foundations of Peace (*The Times*, December 21st, 1940): 'The resources of the earth should be used as God's gifts to the whole human race, and used with due consideration for the needs of the present and future generations.'

Utopian? Only in the sense that we cannot have it all tomorrow. But we can set ourselves steadily to advance towards that six-fold objective. It can all be summed up in a phrase; *the aim of a Christian social order is the fullest possible development of individual personality in the widest and deepest possible fellowship.*

\*     ✪     \*

This book is about Christianity and the Social Order, not about Evangelism. But I should give a false impression of my own convictions if I did not here add that there is no hope of establishing a more Christian social order except through the labour and sacrifice of those in whom the Spirit of Christ is active, and that the first necessity for progress is more and better Christians taking full responsibility as citizens for the political, social and economic system under which they and their fellows live.

# Appendix

## A Suggested Programme

I believe that every Christian ought to endorse the substance of what I have so far said, though, no doubt, many of the details are disputable. I think it most improbable that every Christian should endorse what I now go on to say. But it seems right to indicate how I personally think we should do well to begin. Very likely better ways than these can be found for the realization of our six-fold aim; very likely one or another of my proposals is definitely ill-founded and would, in fact, frustrate its own object. I offer them as suggestions for criticism rather than for adoption, and beg that readers will consider them in that spirit.

Before going on to my own suggestions it may clear the air if I say why I do not simply advocate Socialism or Communal Ownership. Socialism is a vague term, and in one sense we are committed to Socialism already. No one doubts that in the post-war world our economic life must be 'planned' in a way and to an extent that Mr. Gladstone (for example) would have regarded, and condemned, as socialistic. The question is how the planning authority is to be constituted and through what channels it is to operate. We can so plan for efficiency as to destroy freedom; Fascism does this. Or we can so plan for freedom that we lack efficiency. Our aim must be to plan efficiently for the maximum of freedom. Security is necessary to real freedom; legal freedom with economic insecurity may be personal bondage. So much restriction of legal freedom as is necessary to a reasonable measure of security leads to an increase in personal freedom. To put it shortly, we have talked in a doctrinaire fashion about socialism and individualism long enough; it is time to try to get the best out of both. The question now is not—Shall we be Socialists or shall we be individualists? But—How Socialist and how individualist shall we be?

Of course, Communal Ownership cuts the knot—that is the knot in which we are tied up now; but it would tie us up in a great many others, or in one enormous other! Sir Richard Acland argues that so long as there are opportunities for acquisition and for advancement by means of it, so long will economic motives govern society and shape character. But these are only forms of self-interest, and until the vast majority of us are almost perfect saints, self-interest will play a large part in governing society and shaping character. Moreover, not all forms of self-interest are bad. A man is right to demand for himself and his children what is needed for the fullness of personal life, though it may be noble that when he has it he should sacrifice it. Our need is to find channels for right self-interest which do not encourage exaggeration of it as our present order does. Communal ownership would entirely close one channel to it and open others—especially the road to the bureaucratic aristocracy which is an evident feature of the Russian system. The art of Government is not to devise what would be the best system for saints to work, but to secure that the lower motives actually found among men prompt that conduct which the higher motives demand. The law which associates imprisonment with theft leads a dishonest or defectively honest man to act honestly. We must seek to provide such outlets for self-interest while it remains—i.e. 'till Kingdom come' whether here or hereafter—as well as harness it to the cause of justice and fellowship. It is with such a general principle to guide us that we shall consider possible means of advancing our six-fold objective.

1. 'Every child should find itself a member of a family housed with decency and dignity so that it may grow up as a member of that basic community in a happy fellowship unspoilt by underfeeuing or overcrowding, by dirty and drab surroundings, or by mechanical monotony of environment.'

Great strides were made before the war to deal with housing. But we need still more provision of decent flats or houses near the places where men work and at rents within their compass. There should be a Regional Commissioner of Housing (whether the same person as the Regional Commissioner for other purposes or not) with power to say what land shall be used for this purpose. If well-established vested interests are disturbed there should be compensation; but in no case should speculation in land values or vested interests be allowed to interfere with the use of the land to the best public advantage. If anyone has bought land in devastated areas in the hope of making money out of it, he should in any case be prevented from doing this, and ought in justice to lose the capital so selfishly invested. It is to be hoped that the steps taken by the Government in this matter will prove effective. If they do, it will be a welcome novelty! Our handling of problems connected with land has hitherto been very feeble.

When the proper sites are settled, it is likely that State subsidies will be needed in order to secure that the accommodation provided is both good and cheap. These ought to be readily voted; but care should be taken that only those who may be supposed genuinely to need this help should receive it. Municipal authorities have found that this can be successfully achieved. But this subsidizing of rents would be a temporary measure, ceasing when our other measures are operative.

It is improbable that wages will commonly be such as to enable the wage-earner in most grades of labour to bring up a large family in proper decency and comfort. Family allowances—perhaps in the form of food and clothes coupons having the value of money—should be paid by the State to the mother for every child after the first two; the wages earned should be raised to and maintained at a level sufficient for a family of four—father, mother and two children.

While more hygienic traditions about feeding are being developed, it is desirable that free distribution of milk at schools should be universally established, and one good meal should be provided daily at all schools, with a scientifically balanced diet.

2. 'Every child should have the opportunity of an education till years of maturity, so planned as to allow for his peculiar aptitudes and make possible their full development. This education should

throughout be inspired by faith in God and find its focus in worship.'

We now have universal education until the age of fourteen, and improvements are being made, especially in rural districts, to bring this into closer accord with local interests and needs. This should be pressed forward in every possible way. But the 'under 14' problem is generally well understood and is being handled.

If variety before this age is important, it is vital afterwards. Our principle should be that enunciated as a goal by Mr. Fisher when introducing the Education Act of 1918: 'Every citizen until the age of eighteen should be regarded as primarily a subject of education, not primarily a factor in industry.' The word 'primarily' is important, because it leaves room for the development of part time education including in some instances an industrial apprenticeship under the authority and supervision of the Education Authority.

3. 'Every citizen should be secure in possession of such income as will enable him to maintain a home and bring up children in such conditions as are described in paragraph 1 above.'

The present threat of unemployment to the maintenance of home and family must be ended. It has been mitigated by recent legislation, but it must be completely brought to an end.

Yet it is most uneconomical to maintain men in idleness, and the fact of being useless and unwanted is morally the most destructive element in unemployment as we know it. The State should maintain a certain number of works beneficial to the community, from which private enterprise should be excluded, which it would expand or contract according to the general demand for labour at any time. Such works would include prevention of coast-erosion, afforestation, new roads and the like. There is much to be learnt from the Scandinavian countries in this field. But such provision could not cover the ground, and training centres for unemployed men must also be established on a large scale.

4. 'Every citizen should have a voice in the conduct of the business or industry which is carried on by means of his labour, and the satisfaction of knowing that his labour is directed to the well-being of the community.'

The lack of any participation by labour in the conduct of the actual work of production is a manifest sign of the broken fellowship of our economic life. The ideal arrangement would be a revival of something like the medieval guilds on the basis of national charters. An alluring illustration of this was afforded by the Zeiss glass-works at Jena before 1914; I do not know what became of this admirable scheme, and I hope it is flourishing still. But the guilds were sometimes bitter in their rivalry with one another and selfish in their exploitation of public need. Some of our later proposals will include steps towards a Guild Constitution, but it seems probable that the share of Labour in control should be secured by other means. Already, at least in wartime, the great Trade Unions are consulted freely by the Government and have thus acquired a recognized status. Our previous proposals involve 'Planning' on a considerable scale. We now urge that Planning should be the responsibility of a specially created Planning Authority, fashioned on the model of the National Joint Industrial Council, but expanded so as to be generally representative of Industry. This should regulate the Articles of Association of Limited Liability Companies, and should be instructed to secure that Labour is effectively represented on their directorates. Thus the wage-earners in any given concern would be represented, if not directly, then through the great Labour organizations. It is likely that for some time to come such representation would be the most effective. There should also be provision for the nomination by the State of one or more directors to represent the public interest, that is to say the interest of the 'consumer' which should always be paramount. Where the product is of the kind known as consumers' goods, the principle of Consumer's Co-operation may well be followed.

5. 'Every citizen should have sufficient daily leisure, with two days of rest in seven, and if an employee, an annual holiday with pay, to enable him to enjoy a full personal life with such interests and activities as his tasks and talents may direct.'

We have been moving steadily towards a five-day week in industry, and experts are of opinion that to adopt it would increase rather than diminish output, by saving industrial fatigue and with it much wastage of material. Its human advantages are evident. In large cities it may be late in the afternoon before a man gets home from his work for his 'half day' of leisure. In some industries it would be necessary to 'stagger' the days, so that some staff should always be available to keep the plant running. But in most, the whole business could close down for Saturday and Sunday, as some already do. Incidentally, there would be a better chance of restoring to Sunday its character as a day of worship and rest if there is full opportunity on Saturday for exercise, fresh air and amusement.

The principle of holidays with pay has importance in three ways. First, it recognizes the status of the worker in the industry and is a repudiation of the notion that he is an external factor hired for the hours when his labour is needed and no more; secondly, it recognizes that the process of recreation is essential to the quality of his work and therefore to the welfare of the industry; thirdly, it gives better opportunity for that freedom of enjoyment which is necessary to fullness of personal and of family life.

6. 'Every citizen should have assured liberty in the forms of freedom of worship, of speech, of assembly, and of association for special purposes.'

These provisions are of high importance, but do not call for any present action, though perpetual vigilance is needed to safeguard them. In taking care to preserve these forms of liberty the State must, of course, prevent such abuse of liberty by one person or group as imperils it for others.

We now come to the question how we should set about securing these various objects. It is as well, therefore, to recall some of the considerations set forth earlier.

Actual Freedom is realized in fellowships of such a kind and size that the individual can take a living share in their activities. Personality is made real in and through such fellowships, and we need what Maritain has called Democracy of the Person and not only Democracy of the Individual. This has led some Christian social reformers to favour the ideal of the 'Corporative State'. But this swings the pendulum too far. No citizen expresses through his activity in various fellowships the whole of his significance. It is true that to be a Person is more than to be an Individual; but it is necessary to be an Individual; and indeed the fundamental doctrine that each man is a child of God, capable through Christ, the true Son of God, of rising to the height of that status, implies that every man is always more than can be expressed in all his social relationships taken together. The scheme of the Corporative State is therefore as unsatisfactory as either Individualism or Communism. Yet it contains some truth, as do the other two also.

Consequently we should leave untouched the House of Commons as representative of all citizens in their individuality: one man or woman, one vote. But we should not ask this supreme authority to handle directly all the departments of national life. Rather we should initiate a combination of Functional and Regional Devolution.

Few people now doubt the necessity for a development of regional administration. We need means of co-ordinating the activities of County and Borough authorities. And to regional authorities larger powers of administration could be entrusted than to local authorities dealing with smaller areas.

But along with this I suggest that we need Functional Devolution, of which the essential principle is that we set whole departments of national life to order their own affairs—a way of extending effective democracy and checking the tendency of a mass-age to bureaucracy. In particular, we should apply this principle to Education and to Industry.

Thus I would urge the establishment of a real Board of Education, consisting of representatives of the main types of educational institutions and of the public; it would in fact need to contain representatives of the various grades of teachers, or teaching institutions, of local education authorities, of the governing bodies of independent schools; the representatives of the public might be elected by the House of Commons from among its own members, being parents of children actually at school. This representative Board of Education should have power to legislate in educational matters subject to Parliamentary veto.

Similarly I would urge establishment of a statutory National Industrial Council, so constituted as to represent all the main factors in the industrial process—labour, management and dividend-earning investment—and also the consumer, that is to say the general public. This Council also should have power to legislate in its own sphere subject to Parliamentary veto.

We have already indicated·the lines on which it is to be hoped that the educational system should set about its own reform. Can we suggest similar lines to be followed by the industrial system when it is free to organize itself? Here I come to territory where my judgement is of even less value than in what precedes; but I will indicate the direction in which my mind moves.

The early Christian Socialists—Ludlow, F. D. Maurice, Kingsley, etc.—strongly urged, when 'limited liability' was first devised, that this should always be accompanied by conditions securing the public interest against exploitation. I cannot doubt that they were right or that we ought now to remedy the omission. What is required here is an amendment of the Company Acts imposing certain conditions wherever limitation of liability is granted. What should these conditions be?

It is not desirable altogether to eliminate the 'profit-motive'. Room must be made for a reasonable satisfaction of self-interest. But it should be subordinated to the service-motive, so that the initiation or expansion of a business shall be governed more by public need than by private advantage when these two diverge. Above all we should seek to end the right to bequeath from generation to generation a power to levy private taxes on industry in the form of dividends, thus placing on industry a burden disproportionate to the benefit received and maintaining a distinct 'shareholding' class in the community. With these objects I suggest for consideration the following.

(a) Whenever limitation of liability is granted a maximum rate of dividends should be fixed. To secure this the Articles of Association should provide for the allocation of surplus profits to such purposes as (i) a wage-equalization fund, for the maintenance of wages in bad times, even though working-hours may be reduced; (ii) a divident equalization fund; (iii) a fund for extension, as distinct from renewal, of fixed capital, and so forth. The list of objects need not, of course, be identical in every case.

(b) Though it is true, as Lord Stamp observed, that the State already checks unlimited inheritance by Death Duties, this does not go to the root of the matter. He himself favoured the so-called 'Rignano principle' by which those duties would be light at the first transfer, heavy at the second, and annihilating at the third. I should myself prefer the principle of 'withering capital' in accordance with which, so soon as the interest paid on any investment is equal to the sum invested, the principal should be reduced by a specified amount each year until the claim of the investor to interest or dividends was extinguished. The rate of annual reduction would be fixed specially for each enterprise in accordance with the relevant factors involved.

Subject to these or similar conditions, and to the restrictions involved in planning for the basic needs of the less fortunate members of society, there should be room for private enterprise and initative with the free play of choice and interest which these facilitate.

It is computed that three-quarters of the businesses which are started go into liquidation within three years. Frankly, it would seem to be a gain all round that there should be less inducement to start these precarious businesses, of which the extinction must cause inconvenience and may cause real distress. It is important, moreover, to remember that the majority of firms are small. I am indebted to Mr. T. G. Rose for the table on p. 108.

There is a sentimental value in these little firms. But they are a hindrance to progress in the science and art of management, and are the scene of most of the remaining bad conditions of employment. Under our proposals men will be less likely to 'start a little business' because it is more 'respectable' than to become a wage-earner; so much the better. The man of real enterprise and vision will still stake his career on his capacity and will win through. But it is, of course, very important to leave room for such enterprise on the part of men with initiative and 'drive'. Also the units of organization should be kept down to a size making oversight possible to men with less than Napoleonic gifts, and also increasing the opportunities for men of capacity.

Those who accept the existing system naturally ask what compensation on the side of losses will be given to set off restrictions on the side of gains. But our whole contention is that the

STATISTICS ISSUED BY CHIEF INSPECTOR OF
FACTORIES ABOUT EVERY 4 YEARS

Factories According to Size, 1936

| Firms Employing | No. of Firms | % | Inc. since 1933 | Total Employees | % |
|---|---|---|---|---|---|
| 1– 25 | 108,765 | 76·9 | 4,776 | 709,943 | 12·8 |
| 26– 50 | 12,636 | 8·9 | 1,157 | 447,824 | 8·1 |
| 51–100 | 8,738 | 6·2 | 605 | 622,118 | 11·3 |
| 101–250 | 7,155 | 5·1 | 695 | 1,134,048 | 20·5 |
| 1–250 | 137,294 | 97·1 | 7,233 | 2,913,933 | 52·7 |
| 251– 500 | 2,565 | 1·8 | 258 | 885,856 | 16·0 |
| 251–1,000 | 1,016 | 0·7 | 136 | 691,204 | 12·5 |
| 251–1,000 | 3,581 | 2·5 | 394 | 1,577,060 | 28·5 |
| 1,000 & up | 519 | 0·4 | 184 | 1,039,196 | 18·8 |
| Total 1936 | 141,394 | 100·0 | 7,811 | 5,530,189 | 100·0 |
| Total 1933 | 133,583 | — | — | 4,704,354 | — |

existing system is unjust; it is heavily weighted in favour of capital.
And it is to be remembered that under the present system the wage-
earners bear the losses to a great, often a quite unjustly great,
extent; for the bankruptcy of a firm means unemployment for its
employees. A plan for reducing wages in bad times would not be
intolerable if the wage-earners were effectively represented on the
Board of Directors, provided an adequate basic rate were
maintained. Whatever the system, those who have a surplus to
invest, and invest it, must bear the main risk of loss.

If all of these suggestions were carried out it would probably be
more convenient that some department of the Public Trustee's
Office should normally own any business with more than a specified

capital value as holding trustee, its administration being in the hands of a Board of Directors, representing, directly or indirectly, Capital, Management and Labour, in accordance with the scheme set out in the Articles of Association and authorized by the Industrial Council or other Planning Authority.

(c) It must be recognized that the economic problems of the nation are bound up with the problems of international trade. It is in this sphere that unregulated competition produces its worst effects. If we are to establish effectively minimum standards of life and work, we must be prepared for a bold policy of international action. The International Labour Office has done most valuable work which can be greatly extended. Backward nations can be helped with expert advice. But our chief need is to recognize that the world, and in particular Europe, is economically one and that the policies of economic nationalism recently pursued by almost every State have been disastrous to all. It is quite unreasonable and contrary to Natural Order to make political and economic frontiers identical. By recent analogies, if Wales had Home Rule, England and Wales would begin to 'protect' themselves against each other. We must learn to treat questions of commercial policy, as also migration and the means of communication, as matters of general, not particular, concern, to be decided not by national Governments but by an international authority.

As a step towards an equalization of the treatment accorded by nations to their neighbours, and pending the submission of these questions to international control, it might be well for all nations to adopt, as an *interim* measure, a tariff policy based on the principle that in the case of such goods as can be efficiently produced in any country, a tariff be imposed on imports calculated to raise the price of the imported article to that of fully efficient producers of the home-product—but no futher. It is hoped that this would prevent undercutting, and also tend to raise the standard of life in countries where labour is cheap by removing some of the advantage gained by exploitation of that cheap labour. It would certainly involve a drastic lowering of existing tariffs in many countries.

A specially evil feature of the recent economic nationalism has been the search by many nations, including our own, for a 'favourable trade balance.'[1] I know, of course, that an influential school of Political Economists defends this. But we have here a case of the proper subordination of Political Economy to ethical standards. However 'profitable' this policy may be, it remains wrong. It is an attempt to gain advantage at a loss to others; that is one mark of what St. Paul calls 'the mind of the flesh'. Commerce should be and can be a source of gain to all concerned in its transaction. In order that commerce may follow its own 'natural law' in this respect it is suggested that international commerce should be to the maximum extent a negotiated volume of trade, so planned as to utilize to the utmost the productive capacity of all parties to the transaction. Gold might play a part here as a means of adjusting balances when each transaction is complete. Steps could be taken in this direction before international control is established; that such control would aim at a similar result is hardly open to question.

There remain two fundamental factors in the situation about which something must be said—Money and Land.

(d) The private minting of money has long ceased and we have reached a stage where the private manufacture of credit is become an anachronism. Money has three functions: (i) it came into existence as a means to the facilitation of exchange, but it was able to perform this function because—(ii) it is a storehouse of value. Money facilitates exchange because the value transferred in any transaction can be stored up in it for use at another time; otherwise barter would be equally convenient. But so soon as money is owned, it has another function as (iii) a claim to goods and services. It is for this function that it is chiefly wanted by ordinary folk, and it is this function which makes interest on the ordinary loan reasonable. If I postpone making effective my claim to goods and services so as to enable some one else to utilize my store of value in the meantime, it is quite reasonable that he should pay me for this service.

But actual money covers very little of the commercial field to-day. For the greater part of our business is carried on by means of credit.

We all have reason to be grateful for the public spirit and

integrity with which our banking system has been administered. There would not be a proverbial phrase 'as safe as the Bank of England' if its management had not been so conspicuously sound. But the system whereby a Bank of any sort charges interest on credit created by the making of a book-entry and issued for the benefit of the public is evidently open to question. Moreover, the interest of the financial houses and of the producing firms may conflict; and it is wrong in principle that finances should control production.

For with all its three functions, money is primarily an intermediary. This strongly suggests that it should not be possible to 'make a living' (let alone a fortune) out of its manipulation. If one citizen lends his money to another citizen or to the State he is entitled to some recognition in the shape of interest, at least up to an agreed total, because he is transfering a real claim. But when money, or an effective substitute for money, is created and lent by a book entry, as may be the case in the issue of credit, it seems that no more charge is ethically defensible than what will cover the cost of administration, perhaps $\frac{1}{2}$ or $\frac{2}{3}$ per cent. But no private person or group would find here any incentive to embark on it; nor should this power to issue what is in effect money be in private hands.

There seems, in fact, to be as strong a case for converting the Bank of England and the Joint Stock Banks into publicly administered institutions as there is for the State's monopoly of minting money; whether these should be owned and worked by the State or should be Public Utility Corporations is open to question. My own preference is for the latter wherever the method can be followed.

(*e*) The fundamental source of all wealth is Land. All wealth is a product of human labour expended upon God's gifts; and those gifts are bestowed in the land, what it contains and what it nourishes. Most truly the 'Malvern Conference' declared that 'we must recover reverence for the earth and its resources, treating it no longer as a reservoir of potential wealth to be exploited, but as a storehouse of divine bounty on which we utterly depend.'' The land legislation of the Old Testament rests on the principle that the land in a special sense belongs to God. This principle appears in our own Common Law in the doctrine that only the King has full Dominion over land; only its Use is granted to landlords.

There is good reason to insist more strongly on this principle. In the case of urban sites it will lead towards public ownership, for there is little service, if any, that the owner of urban sites can render which cannot as well or better be rendered by the public authority. There is no reason why we should pay certain citizens large sums of money for merely owning the land on which our cities are built. Of course there should be compensation for expropriation, or else a time-limit so long as to meet the claims of reasonable expectation; but the case for public ownership is at this point very strong.

In the case of rural land the balance of public advantage tips the other way. Certainly the existing rights of landlords are excessive if social function is taken as the justifying correlative of rights of ownership; and we are here dealing with a commodity on which the whole public welfare depends.

The primary necessities of life, bountifully supplied by nature, are Air, Sunshine, Land and Water. No one claims to own the first two, or to exclude others from them except on condition of paying a fee. The old principle that justifiable property is a right of administration and not a right to exclusive use should certainly be applied to the other two.

Land is not a mere 'material resource.' The phrase 'mother earth' stands for a deep truth about the relationship between man and nature; and this is most fully developed where a man owns land which he works himself and works land which he owns. But he must own it in the sense mentioned—not as a possessor of so much material resources, but as steward and trustee for the community. Land not beneficially used should involve liability to fine, or, in extreme cases, to forfeiture. But if the necessary safeguards are established, the best results are to be expected from an encouragement of Occupying Ownership. The landlord-tenant system need not be abolished, but it is likely in any case to decay, and the Occupying Owner should so far as possible take its place. If Nationalization of the Land is adopted on other grounds, the tenants of the State-landlord should be given such security of tenure as will make them feel the responsibility and enjoy the independence commonly attached to ownership.

But in no case should land be regarded as a purely personal

possession. How often we hear of an estate being 'mortgaged up to
the hilt' because some heir to the property was a wastrel! It should
be made illegal for an owner as distinct from a purchaser to
mortgage land or to burden it with debt except by licence from the
Minister of Agriculture, who would only grant this either to meet a
temporary depression for which the owner was not responsible, or
for some socially valuable development of the land. Overburdened
estates should be compulsorily liquidated.

Occupiers who are not owners must have security of tenure at fair
rents, with right to make improvements and with compensation on
leaving. All occupiers must also have full control over game.

But a great deal of what is amiss alike in rural and in urban areas
could be remedied by the taxation of the value of sites as distinct
from the buildings erected upon them. In this field, that inversion
of the natural order, which is characteristic of our whole modern
life, is especially important. If house property is improved (a social
service) the rates are raised and the improvement is penalized; if it
is allowed to deteriorate (a social injury) the rateable value is
reduced and the offending landlord is relieved. Taxation of the
value of sites, as distinct from the buildings erected on them, would
encourage the full utilization of the land. There is no need for an
expensive valuation. The owner should be called upon to value the
land himself, the State having power to purchase it at the figure
named or to levy a tax upon it, as may seem more expedient in each
case. Land values, therefore, should be taxed and rated; houses
might well be de-rated. Charges levied on land are quickly
distributed over all which the use of the land facilitates. Death
duties on land, where the principle of inheritance can have a high
social value, should be modified, perhaps by a provision that
payment be made by transer of part of the estate to the Crown on
the death of an owner with a right in the heir entitling him to buy
back that part by a system of hire-purchase.

If all of these proposals were adopted, a great transformation of
our social and economic structure would result. Yet this would
involve no breach of continuity. It would be transformation by
adaptation, not by destruction. Moreover, this method of approach
to the whole problem has the advantage that the various

suggestions can be adopted separately and in varying degrees of completeness. No violent revolution is involved; no rigid system would be imposed.

There is urgent need for thought about these matters now. We cannot return to the pre-war situation. If when peace is restored all the existing controls were removed, that would not put us back where we were; too much has already happened. When peace returns action will be inevitable. We are fighting for democracy; but that crucial action will be democratic only if public opinion is alert and informed.

To these suggestions I add three notes.

1. I have offered the suggestions contained in this Appendix in answer to the frequent challenge, What would you *do?* I deny the distinction here implied between talking and doing. By talking we gradually form public opinion, and public opinion, if it is strong enough, gets things done. Yet it seems fair to ask the proclaimer of principles if he has any proposals for bringing life into conformity to them. So I offer my suggestions as an object of criticism or as a quarry from which a better builder may take a few stones to use for a house better than I can design. I have no special competence to speak of these practical steps towards a more Christian social order. It is highly probable that they are far from the best that can be devised. Very well; in criticizing these someone may find a better way; and at last someone may even find the right way.

2. Let no one quote this as my conception of the political programme which Christians ought to support. There neither is nor can be any such programme. I do offer it as *a* Christian social programme, in the sense of being one which seeks to embody Christian principles; but there is no suggestion that if you are a Christian you ought to think these steps wise or expedient.

3. Above all I would insist as I close that these political proposals must not be substituted for the truths of the Gospel as the mark of the real Christian. If we have to choose between making men Christian and making the social order more Christian, we must choose the former. But there is no such antithesis. Certainly there

can be no Christian society unless there is a large body of convinced and devoted Christian people to establish it and keep it true to its own principles. They can and should co-operate with all who share their political hope and judgement at any time. But they must maintain their independence so that they may judge whatever exists or whatever is proposed with so much as their faith has won for them of the Mind of Christ.

# Notes

## CHAPTER 1

1. R. H. Tawney, *Religion and the Rise of Capitalism*, pp. 170, 171.
2. *Ibid.*, p. 237.
3. *Ibid.*, p. 161.
4. A classical examination of Cyclical Fluctuation and its causes was given by Sir William Beveridge in his *Unemployment: a Problem of Industry*, published in 1909.

## CHAPTER 2

1. 'How can ye believe which receive glory one of another, and the glory that cometh from the only God ye seek not?' (John 5.4).
2. Luke 12.15.

## CHAPTER 3

1. Acts 4.32; 5.1–11; see especially 4 and 8.
2. A. J. Carlyle in *Property: its Rights and Duties*, edited by Bishop Gore, p. 121.
3. *Summa Theologiae* 2–2. Q. 66. A2.
4. *Summa Theologiae* 2–2. Q. 66. A7.
5. Sermon 126. Quoted by H. G. Wood in *Property: its Rights and Duties*, p. 159.
6. Henry of Langenstein, quoted by Tawney in *Religion and the Rise of Capitalism*, p. 35.

7. A. J. Carlyle in *Property: its Rights and Duties*, p. 100.
8. Exodus 22.25; Leviticus 25.35–7; Deuteronomy 23.19, 20.
9. Tawney in *Religion and the Rise of Capitalism*, pp. 128, 129.
10. In the *Communist Manifesto:* quoted by Tawney, *op. cit.* p. 269. The human aspects of the Industrial Revolution may be studied in such novels as *Inheritance* and *Manhold* by Miss Phyllis Bentley and *The Crowthers of Bankdam* by Mr. Thomas Armstrong.

## CHAPTER 4

1. If any reader wishes to know how I should try to establish this contention, I must refer him to my book *Nature, Man and God*, pp. 356–403 and 514–20.
2. *Lectures on Modern History*, p. 12.
3. Ephesians 1.10.
4. 2 Corinthians 4.6; 3.18.
5. Galatians 3.24.

## CHAPTER 5

1. Of course each must be something on his own account to start the whole process of mutual determination. The vice of Determinism is that it ignores this platitude. It says truly, that in a complex—ABC—A is A because of B and C. B is B because of A and C, C is C because of A and B. But if that is all that can be said we have the spectacle of nothing at all differentiating itself into this variegated universe by the inter-action of its non-existent parts. Which is absurd. Q.E.D. But though something must be there before mutual determination begins, it remains true that what actually exists is in its essence a product of this process of determination. Each child that is born brings something quite new into the world; God there creates a new thing, the parents acting for the Creator and therefore being said to 'procreate'. The child is not a mere resultant of his parents' family history. But neither is he anything at all apart from it.
2. Althasius, the inspirer of Gierke, is the great name here. His dates are 1557–1638, so that he was a contemporary of the

more famous Grotius (1583–1643) who used the same idea in his effort to supply a firm foundation for International Law. See my *Christianity and the State*.

## CHAPTER 6

1. Readers of *The Crowthers of Bankdam* will recall the conduct of the senior branch of that family.

## APPENDIX

1. Why so called it is hard to see; for the phrase means giving something for nothing, not getting something for nothing. It is possible only by the export of capital, *i.e.*, involving the other nation in debt.